"Chatham in fact is the only great figure who reached high office not in spite of, but because of, his independence. And because there has never again been a second Chatham there has never been an independent to repeat his record. And with his independence is linked his disregard, amounting to contempt, for consistency. Other great statesmen have deliberately changed from one party to another, admitting that they had changed; but Chatham could denounce and indict a Walpole, a Carteret or a Newcastle as public enemies and presently proclaim without a syllable of pentinence or the quiver of an eyelid that they were either great men or capable administrators who had served their country well and from whom he and all could learn much. He could blast the electorate of Hanover with the lava of denunciation, and the Elbe as an ocean of gore, and presently send a hundred thousand men to protect it and claim that he had won Canada in Germany. For instinctively he knew that his countrymen cared as little for consistency as he did. . . . Results were a greater virtue in statesmanship than adherence to a worn-out principle or article of faith, and Chatham either gave them results or made them realise the gravity and significance of his attitude in controversy."

—From the Epilogue

MEN AND HISTORY

Collier Books ready or in preparation

SIR CHARLES GRANT ROBERTSON

CHATHAM
AND THE
BRITISH EMPIRE

COLLIER BOOKS
NEW YORK, N.Y.

This Collier Books edition is published by arrangement with The Macmillan Company

Collier Books is a division of The Crowell-Collier Publishing Company

First Collier Books Edition 1962

First published 1946

This title first appeared as a volume in the Teach Yourself History Series under the general editorship of A. L. Rowse.

Contents

DA
483
.P6
R65
1962

Introduction

THIS IS NOT A BIOGRAPHY in the proper sense of the term of William Pitt, first Earl of Chatham. Those who desire such will find it in the standard Life (2 vols.) by Prof. Basil Williams, F.B.A., supplemented by the later volume (*W. Pitt, Earl of Chatham*) by Brian Tunstall (1938), to which they can safely be referred.

What is attempted here, in limited space, is a study of the imperial problem of the First British Empire, with which (as the major issue of British and European affairs) the political career of William Pitt, from his entry into the House of Commons in 1735 to his collapse (April 7th) in the House of Lords in 1778, was continuously concerned. That First British Empire ended in 1783, five years after Chatham's death, in disaster and disruption, and a new imperial problem of the Second British Empire commenced with the recognition of the independence of the United States of North America, and with the ratification of the Treaty of Versailles (1783) which registered the victory of France and her allies.

William Pitt was not, as he has often erroneously been called, the Founder of the First British Empire; but unquestionably he saved it in the great Ministry (1757–1761). This achievement closed and consummated the first chapter of his career. The second chapter (1761–1778) was as unmistakably a failure as the first had been a success. Happily for him personally, his death in 1778 spared him the bitter humiliation of the five years which followed his collapse in the House of Lords. Chatham's career, therefore, falls into two main parts, the dividing-line being clearly drawn by his resignation (October 5th, 1761). The historian, as distinct from the biographer proper, has obviously a plain question to answer—the reasons for the success in the first, and for the failure in the second, part. Are they to be found in an essential difference in the character of the imperial problem before and after 1761, or in the character, gifts, defects and policies of the man himself, or in a combination of the two, the problem and the man? The pages which follow supply, in a limited space, one student's answer.

It only remains to add one plain warning. Unless the eighteenth century is examined through the eyes of that century not only will the problems, with which it bristles, be wrongly posed, but the solutions will certainly be wrong also. The constitutional, political and social structure, the categories and idioms of political affairs, the atmosphere breathed and the interpretation of life were quite different from those of the nineteenth century and of our day. The monarchy of George II and George III was not that of Queen Victoria, still less that of Edward VII and George V; the society in which Chatham, Horace Walpole and Samuel Johnson grew up and lived was not that of Palmerston, Gladstone, Asquith or Winston Churchill; and if there was constitutional, Parliamentary or Party government, it certainly was not that analysed by Bagehot, Dicey, Anson and Lowell. The research of the last thirty years has in fact accomplished three things—an exposure of the "legends" which still linger in many books and a reconstruction of the political scene and a restoration of the vocabulary of the actors. Results cannot be altered, but only in that way can they be made intelligible for the jury that in each age passes verdicts on the past.

PART ONE
1708-1761

Chapter I

Prologue: 1708–1735

WILLIAM PITT, second son of Robert Pitt, was born on November 15th at Golden Square, London, and christened in St. James's, Piccadilly. His father was the elder son of Thomas Pitt, famous as Governor Pitt and owner of "The Pitt Diamond" (subsequently sold to the Regent Orleans), and his mother was Lady Harriet Villiers, daughter of Catherine, Viscountess Grandison. The Pitts traced their origin to one John Pitt, a clerk in the Exchequer in the reign of Queen Elizabeth, whose son acquired the property of Strathfieldsaye in Hampshire, thereby founding the elder and richer line, which, in Pitt's lifetime, owned also the lovely country house at Encombe, south of Corfe Castle in Dorset, and obtained the barony of Rivers that lasted until 1803. The younger line drifted westward, and for a century was concerned only with the local life of Blandford, Wimborne, Dorchester and Wareham, until a Thomas Pitt, son of the Rector of St. Mary's, Blandford, born in 1653, and later married to Jane Innes, claiming without adequate proof to be descended from the Regent Moray of Scotland, hewed his way into fame, fortune and no inconsiderable riches in British history, as Governor and "Diamond Pitt."

Of Thomas, Governor Pitt, much indeed could be written,

valuable and relevant to the development of political life at home and of a Great Britain in the waters and trade of the East. It must suffice here to note three or four points, shedding light on the character and achievement of the genius, his grandson, William, "the Great Commoner" and first Earl of Chatham.

The dominating and fierce personality of Thomas Pitt is stamped on everything that he wrote, said or did, and is all the more remarkable because neither Dorset nor Strathfieldsaye Pitts had so far shown force of that arresting quality. And why it should suddenly emerge from a commonplace country rectory is like a good many other things at present quite inexplicable. When William Pitt confessed in middle life, "I cannot bear the least touch of command" he was not only stating the truth, but repeating the leading characteristic of his savage and dictatorial grandfather, with his assertion that "there shall be but one Governor, while I am here" (at Fort St. George, Madras). This "roughling, immoral man," who "to the last made a great bouncing," was an example of the Englishman, piling up a fortune in trade to become one of the group who mixed politics with commerce, "the moneyed interest" with land, and formed in a changing social structure an expanding class between the territorial aristocracy and gentry, administering the homeland, and the traders of the organisation overseas that we call the First British Empire. Thomas Pitt was first of all a vigorous and unscrupulous "interloper" in the affairs of the East India Company, and then as a still more successful servant provided proof that the most efficient gamekeeper is a converted and successful poacher.

Before and after his retirement in 1710 he acquired Boconnoc in Cornwall from the widow of the Lord Mohun whose infamous duel is kept alive in Thackeray's *Esmond,* Down House, near Blandford, Swallowfield, near Reading, and a house in Pall Mall, and endeavoured to reduce "the hellish confusion" in the "cockatrice brood of Pitts" who made his "unfortunate and cursed family." His Whiggism was as violent as was his political independence. A Tory was more hateful and devilish to him than was a Whig to Dr. Johnson, and he roundly rated his son Robert, suspected of wanting "by factious Caballs to put a French kickshaw upon the throne again." He himself twice sat for his pocket borough of Old Sarum, with its seven burgage voters, and let the world know that he "would rather see any child of mine want than get his bread by voting in the House of Commons." Of affection for his sons and daughters he had little, of contempt much, and not without reason. But the fierce old gentleman rightly divined in his grandson, William, "a hopeful lad, who no doubt will answer you and your friends' expectations"; and could he have lived until 1761 he would have claimed that this one alone of his descendants, in his Whiggism, respect for men in commerce, haughty independence, and power of work and dominating personality was not a chip of but the old block itself!

Unhappily, Governor Thomas Pitt bequeathed to his family not merely much money, land and houses, over which they quarrelled like untrained dogs inheriting a parcel of juicy bones, but a physical inheritance which in the next generation developed into almost rabid mental and emotional instability. "There was much insanity in the family" noted the cold-blooded young Lord Shelburne, fifty years later, and, with one exception, every one of William Pitt's brothers and sisters exhibited in varying degrees the same corrosive and neurotic disabilities of mind and body, passed on by the second Thomas Pitt, a cruel and violent spendthrift, to his son and grandson, who made the first and second Lords Camelford notorious for their extravagance and cynical defiance of the moral code of their class. Whether this crippling legacy originated in, and was transmitted by, Governor Thomas Pitt and was aggravated by Lady Harriet Villiers and her forebears, which is more than probable, cannot now be determined. It is the unquestionable fact alone that matters: and the next fifty years were to show how damnably mortgaged the "hopeful" young grandson, William, started on his life.

His boyhood was mainly spent at Mawarden Court (a

gift from Governor Pitt to his son) on the edge of Old Sarum, and at the age of ten he joined his elder brother at Eton. Westminster and Eton were the two leading schools of the day. Had William Pitt gone to Westminster he would have been one of a distinguished group which included Carteret, Samuel and Charles Wesley, the two Pelham brothers (Newcastle and Henry) and, most notable of all for the young Pitt, William Murray (Lord Mansfield). At Eton he had as seniors or juniors Lord Stanhope, Stephen and Henry Fox, Hanbury Williams, Henry Fielding, George Lyttelton, Richard and George Grenville, Charles Pratt (Lord Camden) and Francis Dashwood, all of whom were to find some place, creditable or discreditable, in our national record.

In spite of a good grounding in the classics, William Pitt left Eton with the profound aversion from it and from all "public" schools which sixty years later the poet Cowper expressed bitterly and at length in the "Tirocinium," to be read as a commentary on Gray's better-known Ode. This aversion may have been partly due to ill-health, for the chronicler notes that already the schoolboy suffered from attacks of what was to be the curse of his life—gout.

From Eton to Oxford was the obvious next stage, and in 1727 he entered Trinity College, as a Gentleman Commoner, where he found Robert Henley (destined to be a Fellow of All Souls and a Lord Chancellor) already known for his hard drinking and promising gifts for the law. One year later Samuel Johnson came up as a servitor to Pembroke College, but there was no chance of Pitt and Johnson meeting, for Pitt, abandoning the idea of taking Holy Orders and thereby securing a living, and finding no real nourishment in Oxford studies, restless too and irritable from suppressed gout, had already left for Utrecht and some work there, and subsequently in a desultory mixture of reading and idling at Boconnoc and other houses of his relatives.

Meanwhile, his brother Thomas had married Christian, daughter of Sir T. Lyttelton of Hagley Hall, Worcestershire, and probably through this connection William came into touch with Sir R. Temple, Viscount Cobham of the famous house of Stowe, a powerful and rich veteran in politics and war, and with the Grenville family of which Richard (later Earl Temple) and George had been with him at Eton. The admission to the wide Grenville circle was to be the most important element in the domestic and political life of this dissatisfied young man, and its first fruits were a cornetcy (January 17th, 1731) in the Second or King's Own Regiment of Horse, known as "Cobham's" and later as the First Dragoon Guards.

The Army, not the Church, and then? Military service was not exacting. But the young Cornet preferred much reading in his leisure to the recreations of his brother officers —field sports, hard drinking, dissipation or "flirting with Dolly at The Inn." In the year of the Excise Bill (1733) William had no difficulty in making a lengthened tour abroad, notable for a fleeting love affair at Besançon, in which he neither sighed as a lover nor obeyed as a son, for perfecting his French, which in days to come was to surprise by its ease and accuracy ambassadors and envoys, and for the sight of the junction of the Saone and the Rhône rivers of which perhaps the most famous simile in our political history was the brilliant memory.

When Lord Chesterfield, that shrewd and polished interpreter of the secrets and conventions of the only political society that counted, laid it down that "you must first make a figure in the House of Commons, if you would make a figure in your country" he was expressing an axiom known to every ambitious young man entering public life. That the Cornet of Cobham's Horse was ambitious is already abundantly evident. The Master of Stowe had in the Lower House his little group, "Cobham's Cubs" or "The Cousinhood"; Old Sarum, with its seven voters, as picturesque then in its ruins as it is today, was almost a family perquisite; so in 1735 the first phase of William Pitt's life ended when he entered, in his twenty-eighth year, the sacred laboratory of politics and office, possibly of fortune, power and fame, at Westminster, as member for Sarum.

2. 1735–1742

How was a young man, ambitious and conscious of growing powers, but with inadequate financial means, to make in
1735 that preliminary "figure in the House of Commons"
essential to becoming "a figure in the country"? What was
the administrative system on which political life was necessarily based, what were its principles, machinery and conventions? What was the actual political situation in 1735, and
what were the problems confronting those in power or
their critics and opponents? Two main points are obvious
—and they are fundamental. Great Britain was a constitutional monarchy, governing by a hereditary monarchy,
limited, by law, to sovereigns in communion with the
established, Protestant Church of England, through and with
the consent of a Parliament of two Houses, and at that date
the only constitutional monarchy or state in Europe and the
world—secondly, this constitutional state was not the State
as it came to be a hundred or two hundred years later. And
to understand its conventions and working all the "legends,"
phrases and methods which today or fifty years ago we have
been taught to regard as the essentials of Parliamentary government must be dismissed as positively misleading; and if
the same phrases ("prerogative," "party," "will of the electors," etc.) are found in the vocabulary of two separate centuries they must be interpreted as the early eighteenth and
not the late nineteenth century understood them. To Locke,
Bolingbroke, Blackstone and Burke the language of the authoritative constitutional text-books of today would be as
unintelligible as it certainly would be to Kings George
II and III, to Walpole, Pulteney, Pitt, Henry Fox or Shelburne. In a word, whatever label we may select for the constitution of Great Britain in 1735, it cannot be called a
Parliamentary Democracy.

The House of Lords in the Parliament with whose assent
George II had to govern, rightly regarding itself as a Council
of the Crown, and deriving its authority not merely from its
historic traditions but from the dominating power of its mem-

bers in the structure of society, consisted approximately of two hundred and twenty peers, twenty-six of whom were "spiritual," i.e. two Archbishops and twenty-four bishops of the Established Church, and sixteen were Scottish representatives. Admission to this exclusive chamber was as jealously guarded by the Sovereign as it was by the Chamber itself. For, curiously enough, the "flooding" of the House of Lords was mainly the work of Chatham's son, when the age of "The Great Commoner" had dissolved into a new world of politics and society. Of the two hundred and twenty peers roughly some fifty or sixty were continuously active, although a debate or vote on an important or controversial issue might result in an attendance of a half to two-thirds of the members, while every peer had the right to record, as a Councillor of the Crown, his signed dissent or protest against the decision of the majority. The great lawyers—the Lord Chancellor who presided, a Hardwicke, a Mansfield or a Camden—exercised a strong influence. Even more noticeable was the power of certain families, interlocked by marriage, whose fluctuating "groups" made cells of political action, co-operating with, or endeavouring to displace, the ministers in office.

Of the five hundred and fifty-eight members of the House of Commons, twenty-four were from Wales and forty-five from Scotland, leaving England with four hundred and eighty-nine, of whom eighty represented the Counties (with a common franchise, the forty-shilling freeholders) and four hundred and five the boroughs (on a varying franchise too complicated to be analysed here), with four from the two universities of Oxford and Cambridge. A rough estimate would give, perhaps, 160,000 voters to the counties and some 80,000–90,000 to the boroughs, i.e. rather more than a quarter of a million voters in a population, calculated at about seven millions, of whom two millions probably could read and write.

This, then, was the assembly in which a political apprentice must make his "figure." In "government by public meeting," as is and was the character of the House of Commons, long experience has shown that influence and status depend mainly on two gifts—speech, not necessarily the eloquence which will move a large audience, and the indefinable quality that wins in differing and inexplicable ways confidence in the sincerity and judgment of the speaker. "I expect my ministers to recommend to me measures that they can explain, defend and carry in the House of Commons." That was the task imposed on "the servants" of George II even more than on those of Queen Victoria, the author of the dictum: for they had a master, to all intents and purposes a foreigner, to whom the House of Commons was as unintelligible as it was repulsive. The King's ministers had, in short, to manage the House of Commons—i.e. to carry the measures advised by His Majesty's servants and imposed on, or accepted by, the Sovereign. How as a fact was it done by a successful ministry?

The long supremacy of Walpole was explained by his critics, particularly in the heyday of the opposition and "The Craftsman," as the result of "corruption," by which an unscrupulous minister, using all the resources of the Crown and nation, "as the bottomless pocket of Robin" made and maintained a majority by open bribery. This legend of "corruption" seeped from "The Craftsman" ultimately into "history," the writers of which, big and little, accepted it without verifying the evidence or asking whether it could be reconciled with obvious but awkward facts. For "corruption" failed to keep Walpole in power; it failed to provide the country with stable and efficient ministries after 1742, it failed to save either Newcastle, Henry Fox, Bute and later Lord North, and as an explanation of Pitt's career and achievements as a minister it is plainly absurd; and "corruption" assumes that there was always a majority of members ready to be bought, no matter what their convictions were, which is no less absurd, because the assumption would be an interpretation of the character and mentality of the English gentry against all the available evidence.

But if we substitute for "corruption" the powers of the Crown, in patronage and appointments, we begin to touch both the *arcana imperii* and the conventions of political life between 1730 and 1760. The literature, letters and vocabulary of Hanoverian England are studded with familiar words and phrases, "Whig and Tory," "party," "faction," "patriot," "the public" and so forth, but the serious politician, no less than the Tapers and the Tadpoles, would indeed have rubbed his eyes could he have lived for a week in mid-Victorian or Edwardian Westminster and Whitehall. Railways, telegraphs and motor-cars would not have surprised him so much as the recognised existence of "His Majesty's opposition," of "parties" not only with defined creeds and programmes, but with organised headquarters and staffs and newspapers to bring them into power, of an electorate that could daily read from one end of the island to the other an official account of every debate, and of a Civil List strictly limited to maintain the dignity and provide for the "personal" expenditure of the Sovereign and Royal Family, and of a national budget a hundred times larger than the Civil List in the allocation of which the personal wishes, likes or dislikes of the Crown had no place; and, perhaps most astonishing of all, women voting for and sitting as members with uniform payment of all members, irrespective of religious creed, political principles or sex, and even if the member openly avowed he would prefer a republic to a monarchy, or a "Soviet" to a Parliament.

"Parties," then, in the nineteenth-century sense, simply did not exist in 1735 or in 1760; nor did an organised "opposition" in the form of a group of leaders ready to take office, with a powerful body of supporters behind them, should the ministry be defeated either in Parliament or at a General Election; the traditional broad distinction between Whigs and Tories rested on what was becoming a fiction, between the sections who supported the Hanoverian sovereigns and the Protestant monarchy as laid down in the Act of Settlement, and the dwindling section of those who would have welcomed an Anglican and Stuart prince as the legitimate successor to Queen Anne. It suited the powerful Whig junta, with its grip both on the Hanoverian kings and the central and local government, to brand its opponents as "Jacobite," but if such a distinction had once been valid, it was in 1735 wearing very thin, and "Jacobitism" was more a sentiment than a creed of action, while the leading rebels against Walpole were as soundly "Whig" as Walpole himself. It was the Minister and his satellites, not the German monarchs, whom they combined to drive into "exile." Whiggism as a faith or label was more an attitude of mind than a combative political creed, a hereditary tradition acquired, like your speech, in the class into which you were born and rapidly becoming a "myth" the origin and justification of which no longer correspond with the facts of life.

The true Tories, and there were plenty of them, were the Country Party, with a sincere and profound respect for the monarchy as the mainspring of authority and devotion to the Church of England, an intense dislike of Dissenters and foreigners, of bureaucratic government from the centre and "the moneyed interest," and a deep-rooted attachment to the England of field and covert which they ruled as landlords, big or small, and at Quarter and Petty Sessions. In London they were outside the official ring which made a zareba round "The Court," and they preferred to hunt foxes and poachers at home to hunting for titles, perquisites and places of profit in a capital to which they went without enthusiasm and from which they departed without regret; of the complications of foreign policy and affairs they knew little, and that little mostly wrong; of this German Hanover, so dear to the German sovereign whom a perverse necessity had obliged them to accept, they had as avowed a dislike as they had of a strong standing army. Numbering perhaps eighty to ninety members in the House of Commons, they had deep in their hearts a desire for truly English ministers with an intelligible English policy, and to a man who could say honestly and clearly what was inarticulate in their minds they would respond with surprising loyalty. Such a man had in 1735 not yet appeared.

Two or three other essential points are required to complete the background. The Cabinet, unknown to the law, was well known to all politicians, though it was not the Victorian organ of administration. There were in fact three bodies to which the title was given: the Cabinet Council proper, of some thirty or more members and including the high officers of Church and State, which seldom met, but was useful if some large issue required an authoritative approval; "the efficient Cabinet" of a small group, not necessarily though usually composed of high officers of State, and generally referred to as "His Majesty's confidential servants" or "His Majesty's principal servants" (as distinct from those who were "nominal Cabinet Counsellors"), a fluctuating nucleus not an executive body, but from the personal weight, ability and experience of those who composed it could decide on "policy" for submission to the Crown or to Parliament; while, from time to time, a still smaller cell within the "efficient Cabinet"—a "conciliabulum"—can be detected in which four or five important ministers came to a common understanding. But neither the principle nor the fact of collective responsibility was as yet recognised, and if a minister asserted his independence by voting against a government proposal, his act might be ignored, or tolerated or punished by dismissal, as the Crown or its chief adviser thought fit. Avowed and organised opposition was not in the political code, for that implied either disloyalty to the established order or a "factious" determination of a group to force the Crown into giving its members office—and such action simply was not done. The strongest criticism either of persons or of measures meant no more than a "patriotic" endeavour to free the Sovereign either from evil advisers or from bad advice, in his own interest, assumed to be identical with that of the nation.

All power, in fact as much as in theory, resided in the Crown, and the Civil List, which was the Budget for the year, was "The King's Money," to do with "as he pleased," but subject to national requirements and to the advice of ministers responsible to Parliament. And national requirements meant not only the Navy, Army, the Civil Service—for which specific sums were voted and audited—but the allocation of the large Privy Purse. "Those who dedicate their time and fortunes to the service of the government," pronounced a Whig in 1757, "should be entitled to a share of the rewards that are in its disposal." In other words, the active political nation had of right a claim on the Sovereign's sense of justice and benevolence in the patronage or charitable distribution of the funds available. Incidentally, we must not forget that for three centuries this axiom of our political code has prevailed. What has altered is not the principle but the constitution of the political nation and the amount and beneficiaries of the distribution. To the men of 1735 acceptance of a place or a pension from public funds (English or Irish) was no more "corruption" than the acceptance of an old-age pension or a children's allowance is in 1946.

Professor Namier and other expert researchers into the huge store of unpublished manuscripts have arrived at the significant conclusion that much of the royal bounty and of domestic "Secret Service" money was in reality an organisation of charity, "doles" and "outdoor" relief to needy or unfortunate peers and gentry, to relatives and dependants of those in and outside Parliament, to jobs and places in the Civil Service, to a genuine spy or secret-service expenditure proper, to contractors for government material and the like; that very little was spent on elections, and practically none in buying for cash the votes of members in the House of Commons. The analysis in fact bears a striking resemblance to the budget of the Maison du Roi under Louis XIV, and "the political" nation which bled and fed on the royal bounty at Versailles. In short, "corruption" was not a sinister organisation working from the top to paralyse a free nation, but a continuous struggle to meet the demands of the "political nation" from below, in accordance with prevailing conventions, and of which the hungry applicants always much exceeded the means to meet the unashamed pressure. "The ill-famed, subterranean stream of corruption . . . uncovered and measured proves to have been but a small rivulet and not nearly as dirty as generally supposed." It did not begin with Walpole, and the "system" continued at least to the end of the American War, for North was a far more "corrupt" minister than Walpole, H. Pelham or Newcastle.

So far, then, as there was a party organisation and machine it was concentrated in Treasury Chambers—for there was no other; but not even a tireless and efficient chief, such as Newcastle, with the full powers of royal "influence" at his disposal, could evade the conditions or limitation that His Majesty's minister or ministers must be able in Parliament to propose, defend and carry the measures and policy required: and unless they had this quality neither organisation, "influence" nor "corruption" would do "His Majesty's business" in the House of Commons.

In one feature—the relations between the Sovereign and the Heir to the Throne—Hanoverian England presented a contrast so remarkable as to epitomise clearly the profound difference between eighteenth- and mid-nineteenth-century England. In Hanover long before 1714 rivalry, deepening into hostility, between the Electoral Court and the successor to the government of the Electorate was a recognised fact, and the Hanoverian rulers brought the tradition and fact with them to St. James's and into English political life. George II, as Prince of Wales, continued the hostility existing between his father and himself at the British Court. Succeeding in due course to the crown, he and his queen maintained and intensified this unbroken family antagonism to the heir. Even with a liberal discount from the evidence of Hervey and others, the hatred, reciprocated by the Prince of Wales, of the King and Queen for their son and heir is astonishing and difficult to explain. But, quite apart from its demoralising effect on the social world of St. James, the political consequences seriously dislocated the normal working of the accepted system. "His Majesty's opposition" was not to be found in a defined and organised party, with a defined membership and programme in Parliament and the constituencies, but in "the reversionary interest" (a recognised eighteenth-century term), vested in the establishment of the Prince of Wales, first at Norfolk, and then at Leicester House, and resting on two inescapable facts. The Prince of Wales must, sooner or later, become King; as King he would have an acknowledged right to choose his own ministers, who would then have all the resources of the Crown at their disposal to punish or impoverish those who had opposed and to reward those who had supported the new sovereign before his accession; while the Hanoverian dynasty being what it was, a fresh reversionary interest would start with the new heir to the Crown at Leicester House.

The central point is the Crown and its recognised powers. No one questioned that a new king could have such a ministry as he personally chose and could dismiss from his service anyone from the First Lord of the Treasury to a tidewaiter in a submerged borough, such as Dunwich: at the end of the century, when the insanity of George III made a Regency an apparent certainty, displacement of the younger Pitt and his colleagues by Fox and the Whigs, as soon as the Prince of Wales at Carlton House was Regent, was taken for granted. And what was also taken for granted even more in 1735 than in 1788 was that the organised majority in Parliament which supported the King's government on principle would no less support the new administration—provided that the King did not give his confidence to, or thrust on, Parliament an incompetent mediocrity or a competent but unpopular and distrusted leader, a Wilmington, a Thomas Robinson, a Henry Fox or a Bute.

In 1735 George II was 52 years old; the Prince of Wales (the "Poor Fred" of the gossip-mongers and the ballads) was 28, and in 1738 the birth of a future Prince of Wales and reversionary heir had secured the dynasty for three generations. True, but how long, in eighteenth-century conditions, would George II live, and how long would it take for the baby at Leicester House to develop into the leader of an opposition to King Frederick I at St. James's Palace? Was his gracious mother to be another Queen Caroline or merely the suckler of fools and the chronicler of Court beer? A nice calculation both for middle-aged and young hungering for place or power or adequate maintenance from royal bounty. The ruler could always within reason allot to his friends fields and vineyards and make them captains of thousands and captains of hundreds. But—a puzzling problem indeed—which was the better investment, stout and sincere loyalty to King George II and Walpole, or a promissory note, issued from Carlton House, which might fade before it could be cashed? And things being what they were, that dominating Sir Robert marked how you stood and took opposition or "faction" as ill, as did his sovereign master, under his evil influence.

The problem of government began with Great Britain, brought into Europe, spread to the dominions and stations that made the Empire, and returned to England, for the keys of policy and power were in London. In the Mediterranean were two strategic bases—Gibraltar and Minorca—across the Atlantic in North America Prince Rupert's Land (the Hudson Bay territory), a settlement of sparse trappers and rich furs to the north of an ill-defined French Canada, Acadia (roughly the modern Nova Scotia), Newfoundland, wrapped too often in its pall of baffling mist, an essential base for cod and other fisheries and a potential threat to Cape Breton Island and the St. Lawrence with its French Gibraltar at Louisburg, and then the "immortal" thirteen colonies or plantations along the seaboard, the last of which, Georgia, founded in 1732, straggled along the frontier of Spanish Florida: and so by way of Bermuda and the Bahamas to the West Indies and the Gulf of Mexico, where Jamaica, the Leeward Isles and Barbados flew the British flag, and across the water to the disputed settlements at Honduras and the Mosquitos Coast (named after a tribe, not the malarial insect which ravaged with such deadly result all who lived or fought not only in this but all tropical lands), a treasury of the prized "Logwood," won for the home market by the Baymen with an axe in the one hand and a musket or sword in the other. South America had not yet come into the picture, but sailing east the trader reached the rim of the West Indies in the handful of forts and trading stations of the Royal Africa Company on the Gambia, Guinea and Gold Coast littoral, indispensable for slaves and gum. St. Helena, a lonely watch-tower in the Atlantic, broke for the East India Company the tedious voyages from six to twelve months which touched at the Cape (Dutch) and then by a long slant past Mauritius with its fine harbour and French naval base to Bombay, to Fort William (Calcutta) astride the hazardous and steaming mouths of the Hoogly River, after taking in water, fresh meat and no little alcohol at the oldest settlement of all, Fort St. George (Madras), of which the cornet of Cobham's Horse had heard much from a terrifying grandfather, Governor and Diamond Pitt.

No single government department or single minister was responsible for this loosely jointed empire, unified alone by allegiance to a single Crown. Trade and an inexplicable urge in our people to search out the remote corners that could be reached in ships, far more than lust of dominion or territory, had created this unique joint-stock enterprise of a Great Britain scattered across the seven seas, while the vitality of an expanding trade was bound to add, bit by bit, to the inheritance of the past the irrepressible vigour of the present—and trade increased its pressure on the vested and traditional political interests at Westminster. But unless the motherland retained the command of the sea the Empire would pass from peril to dissolution. "When trade is at stake," said William Pitt in 1739, "it is your last entrenchment: you must defend it or perish"; and, later, he summed up that defence in the undeniable axiom that Great Britain must have "such a superior naval force that even the united fleets of France and Spain may never be masters of the Channel." Exactly. France and Spain—the two Bourbon monarchies—and the more the world map was studied the clearer was the conclusion that far beyond the Channel it was Spain and above all France—not merely at Gibraltar and Minorca but at Louisburg and the St. Lawrence, in the basins of the Hudson, Ohio and Mississippi, at New Orleans, at Cuba, Martinique and Guadeloupe, at Mauritius, in the huge hinterland of Bombay, on the coast of Coromandel and the valley of the Ganges—it was France that mattered. Command the internal sea-lines from Dunkirk to Gibraltar, and neither the

France nor the Spain of Paris and Madrid could reach the New France or the New Spain, but the British trader could and would. For the master of sea-power was like the owner of the five talents, which would by use become ten. Let my Lords of the Treasury, the Admiralty and the mighty territorials of the landed-interest remember that.

What, then, was the right policy for London to pursue towards Paris and Madrid? Orthodox Whig principles met the menace of a Bourbon supremacy in Europe, led from Versailles, with the alliance of the Sea-Powers (England and the Dutch) and the House of Austria, with such other states as could be persuaded or bribed into the system: orthodox Tory principles placed a maximum of effort on the sea and a minimum on land operations, for England was not "in" the Continent but only "of" it; but Stanhope, an orthodox Whig, had made an entente with France the main instrument for European peace, and despite the contradictory and confusing complications caused by Alberoni, Ripperda, the "Termagant" Queen at Madrid, the sleepless pursuit of the Pragmatic Sanction by the Emperor, Charles VI, and the war of the Polish Succession, still raging in 1735, Walpole was neither in the terms of William and Anne an orthodox Whig, nor certainly a Hanoverian Tory. He adhered to the Entente with France, convinced that the first object of a Whig ministry was to complete the establishment of the Protestant Succession in Great Britain, and "in a narrow compass to keep free from all engagements, as long as we can." War or a political situation leading to war would rip open an Aeolus bag of storms.

To all, Whig or Tory, who reflected, one conclusion was irrefutable, and underlay all controversies about foreign or imperial policy. Great Britain, with its population of perhaps eight millions, could not single-handed tackle France, with its population of perhaps twenty millions. Some alliance or European system was essential, and urgently so, if Spain was an ally of France. But what "system" and with what commitments for what objects? If the political world had not forgotten the victories of Marlborough, the indictment in Swift's

"Conduct of the Allies" of a "land war" for selfish foreigners had also burned itself into the national consciousness.

And a new element, Hanover, had in 1714 been forced into the conundrum. When the Duke of Richmond spoke of "our dear Master's (George II) venal partiality for those damned Hanoverians" he voiced what ninety per cent of the true-born English patricians and gentry in London or outside it felt, if they did not say it—except after dinner in toasts. For those "damned Hanoverians" were hungrier than the Scots and had a tighter grip on the Elector's charity with British money; their women as mistresses were surely a divine penance for sin; and their barbarous language was no part of a gentleman's liberal education. But there in northern Germany was Herrenhausen to which the "dear master" went yearly, no matter how much it dislocated administration in London, and there was the Electorate vulnerable from east, south and west, plunging an English sovereign into all the unintelligible complications of a still more unintelligible organisation, the Holy Roman Empire of the German nation. God forbid, indeed, that, as Chesterfield put it, the Crown of a United Kingdom should shrivel under an Elector's cap. The young William Pitt, with no importunate constituents (but a very quarrelsome tribe of relations) to trouble him, had now to decide what to do. His patron Lord Cobham and his "cubs" were on the fringe of an influential Cave of Adullam either already in, or in close touch with, Leicester House. Walpole was their Doeg the Edomite, and in both houses of Parliament the rebels were numerous and influential, while outside London Bolingbroke at Datchet organised, charmed and inspired everyone that was in distress or discontented or desired the place of the chiefest of the herdsmen that belonged to King Saul at St. James's Palace. Without hesitation the young cornet, like the Disinherited Knight in *Ivanhoe*, struck with the spearhead of his lance in the very centre of the shield of the King's First Minister.

Pitt's first seven years were spent in a remorseless attack both on Walpole and his sovereign, because their measures were either un-English or a sacrifice of England to Hanoverian selfishness, or a cynical disregard of English trade, or a cowardly surrender to foreign arrogance ("The Convention of the Pardo was a stipulation for national ignominy"), or, when Walpole was in 1739 driven into war with Spain, a lamentable proof of military and naval incompetence. It is only necessary to note that the attempt to "muzzle" him in 1736 by the loss of his commission simply made him the hero of the rebel patriots and that he led the group which would have exposed by a Committee with judicial powers the "corruption" which so obviously alone kept Walpole in power. Pitt would have impeached and driven into exile this execrable First Minister, while in 1737 he had definitely linked up with "the reversionary interest" by becoming a Groom of the Chamber to the Prince of Wales. The breach with St. James's Palace was complete.

Pitt, in fact, had made good the necessary "figure." The House of Commons fully realised not only that a new personality had emerged from the back benches to the front of the stage, with a power of speech that could scorch like white-hot lava, but that, contradictory as his utterances could be, in some mysterious way this grandson of Governor Pitt was expressing what powerful trade interests in the city and overseas were demanding and what an inarticulate England, mewing its mighty youth, had deep in its heart. In a word, the alchemy of genius perplexed and arrested. A narrow and exclusive society was critical but always ready to discover a new recruit of talent; the flat-spirited and the mediocre in Mayfair were uncomfortable. But force is always unmistakable and will not be ignored.

If therefore the world of Westminster was asking questions, as yet unanswerable, Pitt was learning, too. In 1742, the mighty minister had fallen—from power but not from influence. No Parliamentary vote could deprive him of his experience, judgment and unofficial place in the King's closet, and the galling thing for the new Lord Bath (Pulteney) when the new Lord Orford greeted him with the remark, "Here we are, my lord, the two most insignificant men in the Kingdom" was the truth for Pulteney, and the complete falsity for

Walpole. And when in 1742–3, after the customary runnings to and fro, bickerings, bargainings, intrigues and compromises (with compensations), the Broad Bottom administration was made up, the rebels comfortably shared the places and the loot with the evil men who had deserted a sinking ship; but there was no place or reward for William Pitt. He had no "connection," no little cluster of boroughs to make him "considerable," he was only one vote and a voice that could not be relied on; he had incurred His Majesty's deep displeasure and resentment, and he was in the Leicester House circle, an additional offence to an angry sovereign. For this was how the party system of a free people worked. Nor was it surprising that the "corruption" went gaily on in favour now of those who had denounced it, and that the war was no better conducted and no more successful. Worst of all, the new Secretary of State for the Northern Department was Carteret, a brilliant leader of the opposition to Walpole, transformed for Pitt into the most un-English minister to whom an un-English King could give his ill-advised confidence: for Pitt did not know, nor would have believed in 1742, that Carteret "staked his whole future on keeping the Elector an Englishman" as he understood the term.

3. 1742–1746

Walpole's conviction that a war with Spain would not only destroy the prevailing "system" but open up incalculable and momentous issues for Great Britain, at home, in Europe and overseas, was absolutely right. "It is your war," he said to the rebels in his ministry and to the opposition, "and I wish you joy of it," and both they and Great Britain very soon discovered that "joy" was no part of it. But neither Walpole nor anyone else could anticipate that the year 1740 was to stand out as a landmark. It was notably a year of deaths, the Pope, Clement XII, Frederick William I, King of Prussia (March 31st), the Emperor, Charles VI (October 20th) and Anne, Empress of Russia (October 27th).

The Emperor had no male heir, ready as King of the Romans, to succeed both to the Habsburg territories and the imperial crown, almost hereditary for a male Habsburg. Charles' efforts, the "shadow-hunting" of Carlyle's phrase, had concentrated on securing the succession to the undivided Habsburg territories for his daughter, Maria Theresa, with the hope that the imperial crown could then be continued by the election of her husband as successor to his father-in-law of Tuscany-Lorraine, and then, by a male heir, in due course retain "the Empire" in the Habsburg dynasty. The Pragmatic Sanction which secured this arrangement had been guaranteed by Great Britain, France, Spain, Prussia, Saxony and Sardinia. The Elector of Bavaria had refused, having claims both on Habsburg lands and the imperial crown for the rival Wittelsbach House. But the Elector, unsupported, had little chance of making good either ambition, and had Frederick William I of Prussia lived for two years longer, there might well have been no War of the Austrian Succession.

The new King at Berlin, born in 1712 (and therefore four years younger than William Pitt whom he outlived by eight years), was known, if at all, to Europe as the submissive son of a brutal sergeant-major of a father, who had nearly had him shot for disobedience and "treason," and as the author (in French) of an "Anti-Machiavel," which in reality was to be remembered only as an epitome of what sovereigns and their ministers should not do. But six days (October 26th) after the death of Charles VI this cowed and flute-playing Crown Prince, in command of a superb army and a well-filled treasury, was writing to his friend and master, Voltaire: "This is the moment for a total reverse of the old political system," and on December 6th he was invading Silesia, "to protect the rights of the Queen of Hungary" against all other robbers but himself. And in twelve months' time, France, Spain, Saxony and Sardinia, together with Bavaria, had followed the Prussian lead and torn up the Pragmatic Sanction. The Europe of 1740 had not to wait until 1914 for a Prussian proof that steel was stronger than parchment and that treaties were binding on everyone else but, if necessary, were for Prussia simply "scraps of paper." Neither Great Britain nor Europe in 1740 realised that a new personal and dynamic force had emerged in Westminster and in Berlin. William Pitt and Frederick, usually called "The Great," with only the quality known as genius in common, were to be the only two, in their age, in the first division of the first class in the world of politics. In wholly different ways and with wholly different purposes and principles these two were to make, after much travail, a new age and a new future for Great Britain and for Prussia.

"The darkest spot in England's history is the period of the War of the Austrian Succession," says an expert (Sir R. Lodge), and fortunately it is not necessary to unravel here its obscurities and complications, save where they throw light on the evolution of Pitt's character and growing knowledge and insight. For these eight tedious and unhappy years were often as puzzling to the men who lived through them as to us today, and for the plain reason that, when a system and framework are slowly dissolving, those bred up in the old and disintegrating dispensation do not realise the fact and still less have the essentials of a new dispensation thought out and ready to be the new ends and means of policy. New forces, which always mean new ideas, and events can move faster than the minds on which their impact falls. And so it was for Great Britain and the whole of Europe when Frederick II broke into Silesia in the early winter of 1740.

Great Britain had at once decided to honour her guarantee of the Pragmatic Sanction, but what was she, already at war with Spain, to do with a fleet that could not get at the Rhine, the Oder or the Danube and with a negligible army already drained off to die beyond the Seas?—a difficult question to answer, even if there was no Hanover, lying vulnerable between France and Prussia, and excited at incalculable developments in the German system, to make it more difficult. Moreover, international fictions or conventions, scarcely to be called law, permitted states to take part as auxiliaries without being formal belligerents.[1]

[1] Great Britain, at war with Spain in 1739, was not at war with France until 1744; Spain was at war with Austria, particularly over the Habsburg territories in Italy, in 1741; France was not at war

In February 1742 George II had found in Carteret a Secretary of State after his own heart, who until his forced resignation (November 27th, 1744) was the most prominent figure in Europe. For Carteret, with his brilliant social and diplomatic gifts, great powers of work, and "more Greek, Latin and philosophy than properly became a person of his rank," was the only minister in England with a thorough knowledge of German (so that he could talk to his sovereign in his own language), and, still more remarkable, a thorough familiarity with the machinery, persons and procedure of Europe from Vienna, Frankfort and Munich to The Hague and from Florence to Turin, Madrid and Paris. And Carteret had a comprehensive view and knew what he wanted to do.

An orthodox Whig of the William and Anne school, he saw in France and (a related Bourbon) Spain the supreme menace to Europe and Great Britain. At Vienna was our indispensable "bulwark," which, if "thrown down, left us naked." The Grand Alliance must, therefore, be revived on a comprehensive scale; for Carteret realised that Maria Theresa was determined to maintain her dominions intact, in Italy no less than in Germany, and this meant resistance to Spain and the coercion of Turin (Sardinia): she insisted on "compensation," if compelled to give up territory anywhere. But first and foremost Frederick of Prussia was her enemy. For nearly three years Carteret wove his enormous web for encircling and isolating France, for pulling an unhappy Elector of Bavaria, the Emperor, also, out of the French system, for getting Frederick out of "the war," with Silesia as a reward or bait, for bringing a purely opportunist Savoy over to the Austrian side, and for blocking the Queen

---

with Austria until 1744; the Elector of Bavaria as such and not as Emperor was at war with Austria in 1741; Prussia was twice at war with Austria in 1740 and 1745 but never with any other state; the Dutch were "neutral" throughout, had their ships, to their indignation, "searched" by their ally, Great Britain, and traded with France and Spain and had no part in the Netherlands campaign. When the British and French fought each other at Dettingen (1743) they did so as auxiliaries for or against the Pragmatic army defending Austria from Bavaria.

of Spain in her pertinacity to secure for her second son an Italian appanage, probably at Habsburg cost, and cursing, no doubt, this combination of maternal and dynastic appetite. Three women, as luck would have it, were thorns in Carteret's side, as they were already for Frederick II: Elizabeth of Russia, Maria Theresa at Vienna and Elizabeth Farnese at Madrid; and he was in the position of the juggler who has to keep seven balls in the air and one of the cursed things was always slipping through his fingers, and how to pick it up without losing the other six?

His industry was tireless, his diplomatic fertility of resource inexhaustible, and the King was wholly with him. He probably had reckoned with his sovereign, whom he knew and had measured, but he had not anticipated William Pitt.

Pitt was personally sore and politically angry. The giant Walpole, who held the royal castle of power and policy, had been slain, and there had stepped into his place a "sole and execrable" minister, with the Crown even more completely in his pocket than it had been in Sir Robert's, subservient to Hanoverian selfishness, piling one Treaty and Convention on another (Turin, Breslau, Berlin, Worms and so forth) in the interests of hungry and useless foreigners, hiring with English money Hessians, Hanoverians, Saxons—any wretched German ready to sell his hireling service for British guineas—to fight for alien allies. Our trade was suffering in every sea; our fleet was playing a sorry part, and the one loser in this incomprehensible turmoil was Great Britain. What use was Dettingen and the Pragmatic Army (note the title)? And Handel's *Te Deum* was offensively German music with words borrowed from the English Prayer Book to deceive the public. In a word, the Pelhams must be taught that this betrayal of English interests must stop; an English heart was required in our policy and expenditure, and Carteret (like Walpole) must go—and for ever.

Pitt had become a formidable critic. His technique and his speech grew in strength, and there were few, if any, who did not quail when that lean figure with the hawklike nose, the gestures of an accomplished actor, a voice under an orator's control, and, most impressive of all, that terrible eye with its hypnotic and paralysing brilliance dominated the House. "Pittics," Horace Walpole might call the indictment, but this man was an independent, owing no allegiance to any patron, "faction" or group, and haughty in an almost theatrical assertion of his equality with anyone, be he duke or squire. A poseur, yes, perhaps, for what genius is not? But he said what he meant and he meant what he said. And to the House of Commons, critical and fastidious as it always has been and will be, and with an intuitive sense of the difference between eloquence and fustian, conviction and rant of the hustings, sincerity is a speaker's strongest argument.

And in these three years the narrow political nation mirrored in both Houses of Parliament was puzzled, not merely because it was ignorant, or could not penetrate the fog. We were getting nowhere in this costly war. Clearly there was something wrong, and it must be in the leadership. The interests of England and the Empire were being sunk in a welter of foreign selfishness. And so, Carteret had to leave a sovereign, almost in tears (November 27th, 1744), when we were now at war with France, invasion was threatening across a Channel that we did not command, the Jacobites, so useful to Versailles, were coming to life again, and the Dutch were a broken reed.

Carteret's resignation was not wholly due to Pitt. Sir Robert Walpole effectively pressed for his dismissal. His colleagues, quarrelling amongst themselves, for they, too, could not see how victory was to be won, resented his influence with the King, his long absences on the Continent, in which he gave them little information, until he had arrived at a fresh draft of obligations on which they had not been consulted and his assumption that it was their business to obtain, if necessary, the approval of Parliament. And Carteret not merely forgot the war at sea, but in his complicated diplomacy, coercive as he could be at Frankfort, Dresden, Munich, Turin and Vienna, had failed to take the measure of Frederick II, who would have nothing to do with the settlement of Germany as Carteret planned. No less fatal, he underrated the place of the House of Commons in policy and administration, for Carteret had no "group" or "party" and he suffered the supreme disadvantage of never having been a member of the Lower House. It is an eloquent and illuminating fact that since 1688 there has been no powerful minister of the first rank who, however he ended, did not learn his business by long apprenticeship in that unique laboratory, and some, like Charles Fox, the younger Pitt, Canning, Peel, Gladstone and Chamberlain, only left it to die. Carteret in an absolute monarchy might have been a Richelieu, a Mazarin, a Kaunitz or a Metternich. In the peculiar constitutional monarchy of Great Britain he was a brilliant meteor who blazed and then was quenched.

By November 1744, the Pelham ministry had decided that not only must Carteret go but that Pitt must be either muzzled or secured. But here was the rub. The King (like his grandson later) "dug in his toes and put back his ears." Pitt was both politically and personally intolerable. He had insulted his sovereign, sneered at his courage, and derided everything dear to George and his circle. And he was, also, one of the Leicester House cabal, a groom of the chamber to that insolent, extravagant and scoundrelly son, unhappily Prince of Wales. And had not that equally abominable woman, the late Duchess of Marlborough, just left him (with a wonderful reversion, which never matured) ten thousand pounds, for so "nobly defending liberty," that is to say, for attacking the ministers of the Crown and the Electorate of Hanover, "my beloved Electorate" which Pitt would have left unprotected from attack both by France and that unscrupulous robber and relative, the King of Prussia?

Pitt, too, obviously had been reflecting—and learning. The strength of the sons of Zeruiah was much greater than he had supposed, and the great political machine worked in a most mysterious way; and how to work it required much more than powerful speeches and unanswerable facts. The year 1745 was for Pitt a memorable one, as it was for Great

Britain; there was serious danger of invasion by sea on the south coast; Prince Charles Edward with his Highlanders reached Derby before turning back to meet next year the *coup de grâce* at Culloden: there was a Black Friday in London with a Bank of England reduced to paying in sixpences; Hessians and Hanoverians had to be hired in droves; and French armies under the Maréchal de Saxe were showing that in generalship, numbers and fighting capacity they were much more than a match for the Allies; the Dutch were worse than useless and their constitution was "crazy." Most remarkable of all, perhaps, the Pelham ministry presented George II with a unanimous ultimatum and resigned in a body. The King requested Lords Bath and Carteret to take their place. But support failed, and in forty-eight hours they resigned, Carteret "laughing" as he left the palace. The grass grew up in the morning—it was green at midday—and in the evening it had been cut down and withered. Carteret had always maintained that "with the Crown on your side you could defy anything." But alike in 1744 and 1745 he learned that powerful as the Crown was, in the first and last resort the support of the House of Commons was indispensable. And Carteret never tried again. He was content henceforth to enjoy the finest claret obtainable, the comfort of the classics and the company of his young and charming second wife, and, after 1751, as Lord President of the Council, to season the "efficient Cabinet" with the ripe advice of experience and knowledge in polished phrase.

Yes, 1745 provided ample food for thought—"the most disagreeable year of my life" pronounced the sage Hardwicke. In Treasury Chambers it was noted that William Pitt had ceased to be a Groom of the Chamber at Leicester House and obviously had abandoned "the reversionary interest"; he was now supporting the measures of the Government and no longer indicting subsidies to German and other allies as the wages of sin; in March 1746, as the King categorically refused him any office which would bring him into personal intercourse, such as the post of Secretary at War, he accepted (March 1746) the Vice-Paymastership for Ireland, which three months later he exchanged for the lucrative office of Paymaster of the Forces in England. What did it mean? Was the rebel, in our phrase of today, now working his passage home? Political circles were fertile in gossip, malevolent or cynical or commonplace. The rogue elephant, who could trumpet louder and whose tusks were sharper than those of any other of the herd, was now, as was to be expected, tired of the scanty provender in the forest, and ready to enter the ministerial corral. With a Pelham mahout he would certainly be a very useful beast.

Were the Tapers and Tadpoles right in their interpretation? What Pitt wanted was office; he had learned that the Kingdom of Heaven could not be won by violence, but your value could be raised to a nuisance price; he had raised it unquestionably, and, like everyone else who had neither a fortune nor a "connection," he had done the sensible thing and got his feet half-way up the ladder. What else, the gossips asked, could he do in this workaday world? Pitt himself neither then nor later offered explanation or apology. Consistency he regarded, as did Emerson, as "the hobgoblin of mediocre minds"; and he could and did say that in the crises of 1744, 1745, 1746, an English heart could support measures for the supreme national interest which in different circumstances would be wholly wrong; in fact, it was his duty to do so. It was not office but the country's needs that determined his conduct.

There, in substance, is the explanation. But it is impossible to avoid two conclusions. First, unquestionably, his ignorance was diminishing, his insight increasing. Great Britain at war, not merely with Spain or in support of Maria Theresa, but with France, a great land-power and formidable at sea, could not ignore the Continent, and above all the Low Countries. To wage war simply as an island and fight on your beaches if you were invaded was criminal folly; the enemy, unlike Charles Edward, must not reach the beaches; we must have allies in Europe and they must be supported not merely with money but with men, and Hanover might be a useful strategic base for the co-operative effort. In a land war the point for England was how much should be given in men and money, which must be determined by the enemy's resources and the major concentration on the imperial problem, the maintenance of trade and the defence of the posts or plantations on which it rested. The capture of Louisburg, that superb and unexpected achievement by "colonials" in 1745, was cancelled by the loss of Madras and its results on our Eastern trade. In a word, the argument and experience were teaching a mind willing to learn, that a supreme use of sea-power for imperial purposes involved "containing operations" on the Continent.

The command of the sea meant more than the protection of trade. Behind the command lay a job for an army, to capture a Louisburg or protect a Madras, a Jamaica, or a Guinea Coast. Secondly, neither Crown nor Ministry could be coerced by a single independent individual. Walpole had gone, Carteret had gone, but the direction of policy had remained where it was. The Pelhams and the all-powerful Hardwicke had become convinced that Pitt must be "brought in." Pitt "came in." But the only way to a seat of the mighty was by convincing a very hostile sovereign that he had seen the errors of his youth. Whether Pitt, communing with himself in the silence of a bachelor's chamber, confessed that he had blundered in attacking George II as he had done, we shall never know. But the next eight years are difficult to explain without the conclusion that, even if bygones were bygones, the only way to soften His Majesty's heart was by a tacit proof that the offence was now being purged.

But, apart from politics and psychology, one sinister fact must be noted. From May 1744 to January 1745 Pitt was seriously ill. It was called "gout," which indeed was always with him, but it was much worse than that. It was the first attack of manic-depressive insanity. But neither the doctors nor Pitt himself realised that, in these months of exasperating physical and mental weakness, a cruel fate had knocked with a peremptory warning at the door, and the next knock might be much more serious and crippling.

4. 1746–1754

The periods or stages in Pitt's career do not always correspond with the periods in British history; and the eight years from Pitt's acceptance of office to the death of Henry Pelham seem to have little significance. In reality, what was happening beneath the surface was a pregnant prologue for the world-drama of the nine years that followed the interlude between two wars. Pitt himself emerged from the interlude a different man, though no period in his life is more difficult to interpret with assurance. In 1743 he had broken with Lord Cobham; in 1747 he exchanged Old Sarum for Seaford, a "Newcastle Borough"; he definitely dropped connection with Leicester House, and at the Pay Office he settled down to master the business and to introduce in a very slack service useful reforms for efficiency and justice to all dependent on the Paymaster. It was his first experience of responsible administration, and he learned clearly lessons of great value. He was not a middle-aged novice when he became a Secretary of State ten years later.

His publicised refusal to take as Paymaster the commissions on all public moneys or loans and to hold back for personal profit by investment the sums annually voted for Pay—both practices legitimised by custom—was, and always will be, interpreted according to the critic's view of Pitt himself. Lord Rosebery, in the twentieth century, seems to agree with the "club-land" of 1746, when he speaks of Pitt as "the first of those statesmen who sedulously imbues the public with a knowledge of their merit" and calls these years a period of "sleek silence," "lucrative obscurity, muzzled by a sinecure." And no student of Pitt and his age can avoid a firm impression that, like Mrs. Siddons, who was just herself and not a poseuse when she terrified a defaulting butcher with the tone and gesture of Lady Macbeth demanding the daggers, Pitt could not do a big or a little thing except in a way only too easy to call "theatrical." But what would have been theatrical in Newcastle or Henry Fox was not theatrical in Pitt or Mrs. Siddons. They were made like that. And Henry

Pelham, who knew Pitt intimately, testified spontaneously that "he was the most useful, able and strictly honest man we have," as indeed he was. There will always be plenty, perhaps a majority, to portray Cromwell as a canting hypocrite and Pitt as an insincere Garrick in politics.

The flaming volcano seemed, however, to be extinct. Pitt was little in the House and spoke less. Again, as the Bubb Dodingtons noted, "so, settling upon places, Whigs grow dumb." We have many glimpses of him, with continuous bouts of gout, in country houses, including Stowe, Hagley and Encombe, hearing his fellow-Etonian, Henry Fielding, read *Tom Jones* aloud, writing letters on the joys and beauties of the English landscape in the starched and inflated phrases so unintelligible to us, but as perfectly natural then as was the stiff and formal conversation of Scott's or Jane Austen's gentlemen and ladies to their age. Pitt had more than the fashionable *furor hortensis* of the day; the Paymaster, so scrupulous with public money, was indescribably and discreditably reckless in his own personal expenditure. It was not the extravagance of the spendthrift or the gambler, with one parasitical mistress after another. Pitt stands out in the eighteenth century as a leading figure whom, almost alone, not even the most shameless libeller accused of "protecting" the frail or of finding recreation at the gaming-table while the wax candles guttered their greeting to the dawn. Two women alone figure conspicuously in his life, his sister Ann and Hester Grenville. His extravagance was a sort of financial megalomania, a continuous inability to equate income with desires, no doubt arising from the physical malady latent in his system. It dogged and embarrassed Pitt to the end, and it was the worst legacy that he passed on to his son.

In 1751 the world of St. James and Westminster was completely upset by the unexpected death of the Prince of Wales. "Poor Fred" left debts, and a doting mother of a backward son of thirteen, whose grandfather was sixty-eight, an advanced age for the eighteenth century. The "reversionary interest" had thus collapsed, or would pass to the Regency, if it pleased Providence, as it well might, to remove

His Majesty in the next five years, before the retarded youth, Prince George, had reached the legal age of eighteen. The Regency, therefore, was a political issue, as was also the education of the new heir.

Political "society" fermented and bubbled with gossip and fears. It is significant of the powers of the Crown that men so experienced as Hardwicke and Henry Pelham, Carteret and Chesterfield seriously feared that Cumberland (whose chief henchman was Henry Fox), the fat "Butcher" of Culloden, beloved of George II, a mediocre soldier with a tarnished reputation, would, if sole Regent, use the army to play the part of Richard III and secure the throne for himself or govern England through a puppet and helpless nephew. Newcastle, to whom all unforeseeable possibilities were like a handful of crumbs in his well-aired bed, was in a continuous flutter. But Providence was pleased to give "our gracious sovereign" nine more years of life; and the advent of a handsome young Scottish peer, John Stuart, Earl of Bute, born in 1713, a contemporary of Horace Walpole at Eton, married at twenty to a wife who later brought him a princely fortune, appointed a Groom of the bedchamber at Leicester House in 1750, had for the gossips no significance. Scotsmen were no doubt objectionable as such, but this peer, born and bred in the orthodox purple of Whiggism, was very different from the Attorney-General, William Murray, whose reputed Jacobitism might infect the heir to the throne. The Earl of Bute was not likely, even if he had the chance, to put dangerous ideas into Prince George's dull head. Bolingbroke, also, had died in 1751; but only a few knew of a manuscript called "The Idea of a Patriot King," not yet openly published, and besides, who now bothered about what Bolingbroke wrote?

What Pitt thought is not on record. But if he was troubled, it was not over Leicester House, the Regency or the education of Prince George, but without any doubt over the situation developing in Europe and overseas.

The Treaties of Aix La Chapelle (1748), the result of a Congress that never really met as such, registered a stalemate, for they settled none of the big issues over which Great Britain had been at war for nearly nine years. Pitt coolly admitted that the demands he had voiced in 1738-9 were impossible and were those of a young and ignorant man, and he paid a tribute to Walpole, going as far back as the prejudiced opposition to the Excise scheme, as a wise and patriotic statesman. Subsequently, he paid a similar tribute to the "execrable" and "un-English" Carteret, as his real teacher and "unequalled in the upper sphere of government." Pitt, in fact, was neither the first nor the last to discover that young men can be very ignorant, though they may not be as ready as he was to admit that, in public life, he goes farthest and highest who realises that experience is the name we give to our mistakes.

Much more serious were the clear indications that the whole framework of "the balance of power" had been shaken to its foundation, viewed alike at London or Vienna. For Great Britain, the gravest menace had been France, alike in the Low Countries, in home waters and overseas, and both in the Jacobite business and in Hanover and on the Rhine it was France as a formidable military power able to strike on a wide-flung continental strategic plan that was the core of the problem. The Dutch were useless as allies, internally divided, terrified by France and more than unwilling either to wound or to strike—a small nation steadily going downhill in morale, leadership and resources. At Vienna it was bitterly recognised that they had lost Silesia, for the time, and that for "Austrian" purposes Great Britain was a very poor ally, exasperating in her pressure to get peace by requiring Habsburg sacrifices. What was the value to Maria Theresa of the war at sea, for trade, trading settlements, "plantations" and the like? What did it matter whether the English lost or won at Louisburg, Madras, on the Hudson River, or anywhere outside Central Europe? As Frederick of Prussia was saying, half the fighting might just have well have been on the Scamander and for Troy. Frederick, King of Prussia—there indeed for imperial Vienna was the rub.

The emergence of Frederick was the one really revolutionary element since 1740, for "that bad man" had, if you thought it out coolly, sapped the old systems at three fundamental points: the ramshackle organisation called Germany was now to be a dualism in which upstart Hohenzollerns claimed to be on an equality with the time-honoured supremacy of imperial Habsburgs; the sole criterion of policy was "the interest of the State" as interpreted by its ruler, and "force" was the ultimate instrument for securing it; and in Prussia the "State" was the army (the mechanism of force) and the army was the State. It was an additional item in the indictment that the Prussian King was so able, so remorselessly efficient and so ready to work harder than any of his servants; and Frederick, having secured his juicy joint of Silesia, was now teaching the world one of the first lessons of "Prussianism." As soon as you finished one war, prepare impenitently and persistently for the next. For War is the major industry of all sound political life and only the continuation of policy by appropriate methods.

Another war? To the clear-eyed the black clouds not of one but two wars were rolling up. Count Kaunitz, born in 1711, the ablest head in Austrian service since Prince Eugène of Savoy, who had studied Europe at Turin, Aix-la-Chapelle and Paris and now the chief and trusted adviser of his sovereign at Vienna, had convinced himself that, in the interests of what he called, with wearisome iteration "the August House of Austria," the stolen Silesia must be recovered, and that the Maritime Powers were no use for this purpose, but that a tourniquet of Austria, France, Saxony, Russia and Sweden could reduce the insolent robber to his proper place in the Germanic system. Versailles and Vienna in alliance! a diplomatic revolution, indeed, for there is no one so truly revolutionary as the inheritor of a gnarled tradition who starts thinking for himself. And Kaunitz, in his stuffy and overheated chancellery (which did not prevent him from living to 1792) was now working like a beaver to "encircle" Prussia; and Frederick, *toujours en vedette*, knew he would only save Prussia from dismemberment by force—

and the right alliance, acting at the right moment, as in 1740.

Neither in London nor in Versailles did the governments want another war, but how could they stop the steadily rising sap in their respective peoples? In India, on the West Coast of Africa, in the West Indies, and, most of all, in North America, expansion and ambition could not be drugged by indifference, ignorance or timidity at headquarters. Madras and Louisburg were most uncomfortable red-lights for both the British and French governments. For if the French, already controlling one vital entrance and waterway—the St. Lawrence—pushed down from Montreal, with fierce Indian tribes as their allies, to the headwaters of the Ohio and so to its junction with the Mississippi, and met there French coming up from New Orleans, while a chain of forts and trading-stations blocked the exits westwards from the Allegheny Barrier, what was the future of the thirteen Plantations, discordant but seething with life, between the Alleghenies and the Atlantic? Martinique and Guadeloupe in the West Indies, together with Cuba (under a Bourbon Spain with two Family Compacts in its archives), threatened an indispensable British trade, as did Goree on the West Coast of Africa; and how was the East India Company to maintain what it had won by a century of effort and to combat with its own resources the insight and energy of a Dupleix, a Lally and a La Bourdonnais, in the Carnatic, the Deccan and the basin of the Ganges?

Since Pitt had become Paymaster the imperial problem was passing from scattered, if locally important, conflicts in two hemispheres into two capital issues: was this vast American continent to be English in culture, speech and institutions, and how could that be if France controlled the St. Lawrence and Cape Breton Island at one end and New Orleans and the Gulf of Mexico at the other? Was the vast Indian Peninsula, and a disintegrating Mogul Empire, gradually to pass under French Mayors of the Palace, directing the policy and commanding the resources of a galaxy of native states and princes?

In a single sentence, in two hemispheres either Great Britain or France must come out on top, for, paradoxical as it sounded, there was not room for both, huge as the spaces were. Capitulation could avert a collision; but if the men of either side on the spot refused capitulation, then it must be war, with defeat or victory as the result, and the key to victory lay in the command of the indivisible and unifying sea.

Newcastle, now in control of foreign policy, had seen with dismay the virtual collapse of the Grand Alliance of 1689 and 1702 and was convinced it was the first interest of Great Britain to restore it to a vigorous efficiency. France, of course, was both the chief enemy and danger—a France at present in alliance with Prussia. With the same industry that he "managed" boroughs and borough-mongers he was now trying to repeat the diplomatic strategy of Carteret; the Archduke Joseph, elected King of the Romans, would secure the imperial crown for the Habsburgs, a network of sub-sidised German states would separate France from Prussia, a subsidised Russia to the east would prevent Prussia from another "Silesian raid," and Vienna must make the Low Countries (Belgium) safe for the Dutch and against French invasion. Two wars would thus be averted.

Newcastle, supported by George II, went a long way to success, but the plan broke down for two main reasons: "the August House of Austria" refused to make the Barrier fortresses in the Austrian Netherlands effective and the Dutch were neither willing to pay for their maintenance nor to fight; the danger from France could be met by Versailles and Vienna agreeing to share the hegemony of Europe, be-cause a revived Grand Alliance to maintain peace would not restore Silesia to its lawful ruler; at home his brother, Henry Pelham, First Lord of the Treasury, nursing by strict economy Great Britain from convalescence to financial health after seven years of costly war, like Walpole, wished to keep clear as long as possible of Continental "engagements," and this endless chain of proposed subsidies was fatal to a balanced Budget and had to run the gauntlet of a peevish but English

House of Commons; and the silent Paymaster-General was growling with his chief and beginning to show his dangerous teeth. Where, Pitt was asking, did the Empire come into this complicated plan? The subsidies had much better be spent on an inadequate navy, and more effective help to Russia and a check to Prussia would be a strong squadron (which we had not got) in the Baltic. The "efficient Cabinet," of which Pitt was not a member, shared these misgivings, and it would take all Henry Pelham's skill to defend and secure Newcastle's elaborate scheme. A ground swell of revolt—"no land war, no subsidies"—was in fact beginning to run deep and strong.

Fate unexpectedly intervened. On March 6th, 1754, Henry Pelham, the Head of the Government, and the only Commoner in the Cabinet, died. The Ministry must be reconstructed; and if Newcastle became First Lord of the Treasury and Head, who was to lead for the new Ministry in the House of Commons? Newcastle could provide a disciplined majority, but all experience showed that the House would not be led from the Lords but must have a ministerial leader in whom it had confidence and who had his own access to the Royal Closet. There were three, and only three, possibilities: William Murray, the Attorney-General; Henry Fox, Secretary at War; and the Paymaster-General, William Pitt—first-rate speakers to whom the House always listened with respect and, in the case of Pitt, with fear and admiration. Combined in a trio, they would make a stronger Treasury Bench than had been seen since 1714. Pitt was seriously ill at Bath and unable to travel to London, to which he had to write too late. It was the first, but not the last, time when his mental malady, aggravated by gout, crippled him at a critical point in his career; and when he had sufficiently recovered, the Ministry had been reconstructed; he remained where he had been, as did Henry Fox, while William Murray was about to insist on becoming Lord Chief Justice (as Lord Mansfield) and to leave for ever the Lower for the Upper House. He could be a big political figure, but he rightly knew that he could be a still bigger figure in law—and not exposed to Pitt's irony and invective. After April 1754 it was not only George II who had reason to say in the oft-quoted remark: "Now I shall have no more peace."

5. 1754 (April)–1756 (November)

This year, 1754, is a turning-point in Pitt's career. Had he died at Bath he might have had a few lines in the text-books as a brilliant *frondeur*, a notable orator, with a crushing power of attack, and an efficient administrator in an office of the second rank, but at the age of forty-six had shown no sign of real statesmanship. A deep impression of personality on contemporaries with no achievement on record to confirm the impression very soon evaporates. Posterity cannot re-create or meet the personalities of the past unless, which is very rare, an artless Boswell turns them into literature. Pitt would have had the testimony of Horace Walpole, and a three-line note giving birth and death by an editor.

Newcastle explained with over-elaborate politeness and at length that His Majesty's veto was the reason why the Paymaster could not be promoted to an office more suitable to his abilities and service. Pitt, still physically depressed, obviously angry, and still more disappointed and humiliated, confessed that "the load of His Majesty's displeasure was too great to move under." Was this cry of the heart a confession, like that of Mirabeau's, of punishment for "les fautes de ma jeunesse," and were his bitter attacks both on Hanover and the King never to be forgotten or forgiven? Two comments of shrewd observers are very relevant: "Pitt has no health," wrote Horace Walpole, "no party and, what in this case is allowed to operate, the King's negative"; "his (Pitt's) passion is not money (wrote George Grenville); it was ambition, power of which he had no share . . . they (Newcastle, Hardwicke and Co.) should have made him well with the King, who was his enemy, which they had never taken the least care to do."

Newcastle, in 1748, expressed his "determination never to have any minister in my Department who tells me that he is wiser than I am," and was uncertain whether he feared Pitt in opposition more than in the "efficient Cabinet" in which he rightly guessed he would be the dominating force. The King's dislike of Pitt is beyond question. Whether Newcastle, with Hardwicke, could have forced a very obstinate sovereign to give way, had he been convinced that Pitt was indispensable, cannot be answered with certainty; nor do we know whether Pitt himself believed that Newcastle had honestly tried and failed, or was using the Sovereign's hostility to screen, in the manner of Spenlow and Jorkins, his own determination not to share power with anyone obviously abler than himself. Whatever the true interpretation may be, the one thing that is certain is that, if Pitt had become a Secretary of State in the summer of 1754, the history of the next two years would have been very different, and there might never have been the Seven Years War as history records it. Not for the first, or the last, time Great Britain paid a cruel price for years wasted or misused by mediocrity in office.

But while the political world continued to speculate on the future of Fox and Pitt, it got a fresh surprise in the engagement (September) and marriage (November 16th) of Hester Grenville to the Paymaster-General. This had the full approval of the Grenvilles, beginning to be known as "The Cousinhood" or "The Family," headed by Richard, now master of the historic and stately Stowe, determined to secure for himself an Earldom and Knighthood of the Garter, in recognition of merits, not apparent, then or since, to anyone but himself.

Pitt had first known Hester as a girl of fourteen. Why their marriage was deferred until he was forty-six and she was thirty-three—health or lack of money on his side or failure in both to discover a bond deeper than friendship—will never be known. But this in 1754 was a marriage of true love, and for William Pitt it proved to be, at a critical phase, the most decisive element in his life and career.

Let it be said once and for all that Hester Grenville has been rightly called one of the suppressed characters in our history; for after Queen Caroline she was in reality the ablest woman in politics of her day. Her portraits by Hudson reveal both charm and breeding in a graceful head and slim figure, but fail to convey the brains and strength of character that she almost proudly concealed from all but a small circle. From the start to the close of her wedded life she was an inspiration and a comfort to a husband of whose devotion she was assured, but whose physical disabilities must have "gey ill to live wi'"; and the next twenty-five years were to show that she could be the best of mothers, nurse, secretary, bailiff and accountant, wrestling with the increasing difficulties of her husband's reckless extravagance, with tiresome and exacting brothers, with a voluminous correspondence and inquisitive or importunate visitors, but always cool, dignified and mistress of herself. Thomas Coutts (1735–1822), the founder of the famous banking firm, who knew all the notables of a long life, called my lady Chatham, for whom he had much affectionate admiration, "the cleverest *man* of her time in politics and business." And fate, if it imposed a heavy burden on her through the brilliance of unexampled fame and the gloom of failure and defeat, was kind in its rewards; for Hester lived to see her beloved second son Prime Minister for sixteen years to the sovereign who had denounced his father as a "trumpet of sedition," before she joined in 1803, in the North Transept of Westminster Abbey, the husband to whom she had once written: "my fame, my pride and my glory are centred in you."

Marriage restored Pitt's health, banished his depression and refired his ambition. He came back to Westminster at the end of 1754 with but one aim. He would show the Newcastle group and their disciplined Janissaries what manner of man he was. Even more than Walpole and Carteret, Newcastle must go and, in the words of twenty years hence, "the throne be instructed in the language of truth." Achilles, in fact, was about to emerge from eight years of silence and his voice of terror and defiance would find an answer beyond the trenches of the Treasury Bench in every English heart. War was at hand; and there was only one man who could save England, the Paymaster-General. He knew it, and soon they

—or rather *he* in the Treasury, "an overmighty subject"— would know it, too, from "the cries of a bankrupt people."

The next two years in home politics with their negotiations, intrigues, cross-currents, combinations, fears and correspondence, covering acres of print or unprinted paper would easily fill a book of their own, but the really important results, extricated from a jungle of detail, are clear. Newcastle's plans to "manage" the House of Commons through a second-rate diplomatist (Sir T. Robinson) with neither the qualifications nor the experience to lead or persuade broke down in six weeks, under the drum-fire of Henry Fox, with his own reasons for feeling sore (in spite of admission to the Cabinet, though not to the conciliabulum or "Inner Clique"), and not prepared to sell his unquestionable abilities except for the price that his cold-blooded ambition regarded as adequate, and of William Pitt, surpassing himself in power to indict and to ridicule; while the "silver-tongued" Murray refused to "suffer" weekly from the scorching flame of the Paymaster's tongue. Racked by daily palpitations at what might happen if Fox and Pitt combined and linked up "the Cumberlands" with Leicester House, where with every month "the reversionary interest" grew stronger, as the King became older, Newcastle was being taught what Parliamentary government, under mid-eighteenth-century convention, implied. He must consent to share his power, and he must secure either Pitt or Fox. To Hardwicke's soundings Pitt made it perfectly clear that he would never speak from a brief, that he must have an office and a place in "the efficient Cabinet" where policy and measures were decided, and that, while some limited subsidies might be necessary with due consideration for Hanover, our main effort must be not in a Continental war but for the Empire and trade overseas—the Mediterranean, the Atlantic, and even in the Indian Ocean.

Newcastle's reply was to ally with Fox, who became (November 1755) a Secretary of State and took over "the conduct of the House of Commons" in order to force the subsidy Treaties through, and on November 21st Pitt, Legge (the Chancellor of the Exchequer) and George Grenville were dismissed from their respective offices. For Pitt, whose first son was born in the same month, it was a loss of £4,000 a year, not compensated for by the £1,000 promptly offered him by his brother-in-law, Richard, Earl Temple, one of the many instances of Pitt's readiness to accept financial help from relatives and friends, which he seemed always to regard as a duty and a privilege on their part to provide.

The future of Newcastle's ministry, with which Fox had now identified himself, and of Great Britain was not to be settled by kaleidoscopic combination and recombinations at Westminster or in the Royal Closet, but by events, seemingly beyond the control of London or Versailles, heralding doom like the strokes of a tragic Destiny. In 1754, Colonel George Washington, a Virginian landowner, had been driven out of Fort Duquesne by the French, and the failure of a Congress at Albany, angry at the restoration of Louisburg (now being refortified) to France in 1748, to unite the Thirteen Colonies in any common effort for defence or administration had emphasised the two great dangers—the French plan for uniting the St. Lawrence, the Ohio and the Mississippi by a chain of forts west of the Alleghenies and the jealous rivalries of the Thirteen Colonies preventing united action. The Ministry at home had sent out General Braddock with a small force, but in July it had been ambushed on the Monongahela, cut to pieces and Braddock killed. The naval measures under Boscawen and Hawke had only succeeded in angering the French, and damaging their trade, so that when Frederick, who "feared the Russians far more than he feared God," and alarmed at our subsidy treaty with the Czarina, obtained by lavish bribery, agreed by the Convention of Westminster (January 16th, 1756) to a mutual guarantee of the Prussian Kingdom and the Hanoverian Electorate, Kaunitz obtained his final argument for a new European system, and the antagonism for three centuries of Bourbon and Habsburg was ended by the First Treaty of Versailles (May 1st, 1756).

If in the same month (May 18th) France was formally at war with Great Britain, Frederick knew that France, Russia and "Austria" were united not merely to recover Silesia but to dismember his kingdom. His one and only ally now was a Great Britain shivering for six months in the fear of a comprehensive invasion and crying out for protection by any Germans or Swiss whom money could buy. Almost worse, Minorca had been lost (June 28th). Warned as far back as the end of 1755 that the French were planning a stroke at this strategic base in the Mediterranean, the Ministry sent (April 7th), too late, too small a squadron and under the wrong man, the hapless Byng.

Fierce indignation now inflamed panic, in which the loss of Oswego seemed almost a trifle. Newcastle, terrified at the prospect of impeachment by Pitt, coming to be known as "the Great Commoner," pleaded for "something to be done at once, until it could be seen what really might be done," had next on his hands the resignation of Henry Fox (October 1756), refusing "to be treated like a dog" any longer; and then came the news, which startled Westminster and Mayfair, that Pitt's chariot had really been seen (October 21st) outside the door at St. James's Palace, which led to the private apartments of the Countess of Yarmouth, no Madame de Pompadour, the maker of ministries, but a faithful transmitter of what important personages who could not see the King were anxious should reach the ear of His Majesty. Newcastle promptly resigned, and on November 15th Pitt kissed the hand of a sovereign who had accepted the Duke of Devonshire as his First Lord of the Treasury, and gave him, with tears in his eyes, the Seals of a Secretary of State for the Southern Department. Hanover by this arrangement at least would not be under this man, forced by a terrified nation on a most reluctant ruler. Pitt had at last arrived.

The Seven Years War had really begun in the first week of September, when Frederick, against our repeated advice to hold his hand, marched into Saxony to break the encirclement by his foes, before they could bring their united forces into the field. By the Convention of Westminster, the two wars, separate in their origin and objectives, of France with Great Britain and of Prussia with the House of Austria, had now merged into a single world-wide struggle which would decide the future of the British Empire and of the European state system, revolutionised by the reversal of the historic alliances. Victory for Frederick meant his survival with his dominions intact; victory for Great Britain meant an intact and expanding Empire based on British supremacy in North America and India. The defeat of either of the partners meant the defeat of both.

How Frederick must fight his war was obvious: how Great Britain was to fight her war was anything but clear. Why had the seven years from 1739 to 1748 ended in a stalemate, and the war of 1702 to 1713 in a decisive victory? Were we now to strive for another Blenheim, Ramillies, Oudenarde and Malplaquet, and where was our Marlborough? Was Prussia to be saved on the St. Lawrence, or North America to be won on the Weser and the Elbe? Hard questions indeed.

The nation, in 1756, was depressed as it had never been depressed before. The testimony of contemporaries is impressive alike in the sincerity and unanimity of the judgments expressed. As the young Lord Shelburne records, "I have never been able to find there was a single man in public affairs who did not believe we were utterly ruined," and confirmation lies in the letters of Horace Walpole, Chesterfield and Gray. There was one exception, the new Secretary of State, the man "with an eye that would cut a diamond," and with a confidence in himself surpassing that of Nelson, and a disregard for consistency unequalled in its superb indifference. Pitt in 1756 had indeed "scoured his anti-Hanoverian trumpet," and denounced the Elbe as an "ocean of gore." But Pitt in power was a different man from Pitt vainly hammering at the door of high office. He probably knew in December 1756 as little as the nation which felt he was the one man who might save them, as to how exactly he was going to do it. But it could and must be done.

Chapter II

The Great Ministry: 1756–1761

ONCE AGAIN, IT MUST BE NOTED that the phases in Pitt's career do not correspond with the phases in our national history. "The Grand Ministry" commencing in December, 1756, was nominally under two successive First Lords of the Treasury, the Duke of Devonshire (until April 1757) and the Duke of Newcastle (July 1st, 1757), but for his day and ever since it was the ministry of Pitt; and it ended in October 1761 with Pitt's resignation. It was cut across by the death of George II and the accession of his grandson, George III, in October 1760. In our national history the Seven Years War ends a chapter with the Treaty of Peace in 1763, when a new epoch opens. But for Pitt, the first chapter ended in 1761, and the second half of his career begins in the autumn of that year. The national and the personal phases then combine into a united evolution.

"A grain of sand in a man's system and empires fall and perish" is a conclusion that at times seems most uncomfortably true; for to all endeavouring to find a meaning in the sequence of events that is called history it is disconcerting to realise, and exceedingly difficult to appreciate exactly, the effect of a prolongation or termination of this life or that in a specific period, or the limitations on, or the opportunities to, genius by the lives or deaths of those with whom it is in contact or with whom it is called upon to work. Had Ferdinand VI of Spain not died in 1759 and been succeeded by Charles III from Naples, had George II died in 1758 or lived until the end of 1762, had the Czarina Elizabeth not died in 1762 and been succeeded by the half-mad Czar Peter, in each case the physiology of an individual being the determining factor, Pitt's career and the history of the British Empire (to go no wider) would certainly have been very different from what they actually were. The Seven Years War was certainly not simply the work of three women, the Empress Maria Theresa, the Czarina Elizabeth and Madame de Pompadour, *"les trois catins,"* exasperated into war by the bitter insults of Frederick of Prussia, any more than the Persian War was the outcome of a curtain-lecture by Atossa, or the Reformation in England due to "the Gospel Light that dawned (if it did dawn) in the eyes of Anne Boleyn." But the personal resentment and influence of the three august ladies in 1756 cannot be dismissed as negligible or irrelevant.

And so with Pitt. His principles, his temperament and his physical maladies and handicaps are elements, appreciable but not measurable by a precise and confident analysis, in the parallelogram of forces that made the world situation. His admission to high office was the result of an upsurge of national feeling combining with the impress of an individual's career, unique at the time and ever since. "Unattached to any party, I am and wish to be entirely single"—a later expression of his position—was true from his entry to the House of Commons until his death. He could co-operate with successive groups, Cobhamites, Grenvilles, Cumberlands, Leicester House, but he broke with them all in turn, as he did with the groups after 1762; he had no "connection," he never attempted to form one or to build up, as he might easily have done, a "faction" with a voting strength of its own demanding "consideration" and its share when office and places were settled by hard bargaining; if, before and after 1761, there was a "Pittite group," it was not made by Pitt but by individuals forming up behind a leader who inspired but did not organise them to follow him. In the dark days of 1756, accused of aiming at becoming a "sole minister," he replied that what he wanted was not a "sole minister" but "a system" and "decision." Party government, as Newcastle understood it or as Burke later ideally defined it, he either rejected or despised, as contrary to any sound national system based not on "men," combining to force themselves on the Crown, but on "measures" which had nothing to do with the principles or manœuvres or objects of "party." A national government could, indeed ought to, consist of men from any and every party or it would not be national, serving under a sovereign who must in theory and in fact be free from all party pressure or obligations. This was Pitt's conception of a "Patriot King"—in words not so different perhaps from Bolingbroke's but in practice totally different, for policy and measures would be determined by one master mind—himself.

This independence, unique, puzzling, inspiring, exasperating, was an immense source of strength, earning rightly for Pitt the title of "the Great Commoner," particularly in a period of national crisis, when it coincided with an inarticulate but irresistible movement in national sentiment; but it was, also, an immense weakness, if the independent leader no longer expressed what a majority felt and his "measures" were really those of a party, which must fight as a party to convince opponents that they were really national. A leader in that case, without a party, but in battle against an organised party, was perilously like Swift's unarmed man in his shirt against six armed opponents. And Pitt's weakness as an independent was not only grievously accentuated by his ill-health but by his arrogance, his Olympian disdain, his irritability and a singular incapacity to understand or manage important individuals or the rank and file of political life. Pitt inspired fear, admiration, devotion, resentment and even hatred in persons whom he had offended or thwarted, but never affection or love. The political world never saw him as Hester Grenville and his children alone knew him; they only saw the haughty figure, always in full peruke and dress,

with the aquiline nose and that terrible eye, proud, dominating and unbending, passing through their midst like that
Dantean angel whose mind was fixed on other things.[1]

It was obvious to everyone that the Devonshire ministry
could not last. The nominal leader was a mediocrity, of ducal
rank, but Pitt had no solid core or "connection" to make it
really an efficient "system": at the Admiralty his brother-in-
law, Earl Temple, even more arrogant than Pitt and without
his brains, and the Chancellor of the Exchequer, Legge, made
his "party"; the King was hostile, speaking of Pitt and his
colleagues as "those scoundrels" and resenting with good
reason Temple's insolence and importunity to secure "the
Garter"; Holdernesse regularly betrayed cabinet secrets to
Newcastle and Fox, in real command of the only party organisation that existed, and waiting confidently for the down-
fall of those who had turned them out; and Pitt was racked
with gout. No one was surprised, therefore, when Temple
(April 4th) and then Pitt himself (April 6th) were dismissed.
The prologue to a grand drama was a shabby and disappoint-
ing failure.

There followed the most extraordinary episode in our
political history, when for eleven weeks, in a war going very
badly, Great Britain was without an administration and
Holdernesse, who had not been dismissed or resigned, was
the sole executive for the British Empire. Whitehall and
Westminster were like an ant-heap stirred to its depths; the
Tapers and Tadpoles, the Rigbys and Bubb Dodingtons and
Stones with peers "as plentiful as tabby cats, in point of fact
too many," chattered, negotiated, bargained and intrigued.
The political and commercial nation, however, made one
conclusion clear, through a shower of "gold boxes and free-
doms," that Pitt must return to power: it was no less clear

[1] "ma fe' sembíante
d'uomo cui altra cura stringa e morda
che quella di colui che gli è davanti"—
(But looked like a man whom other cares compel and incite,
rather than those who stand before him.)
Dante—Inf. ix, 101–103.

that Newcastle ("the Master of many legions") could not be left out, and so, at last, the Newcastle-Pitt Ministry—a mosaic of all the interests including Leicester House—was formed by the end of June. Pitt returned to be Secretary of State for the Southern Department, with an implied direction of the war; Newcastle as First Lord of the Treasury recovered the congenial duty of managing the House of Commons and patronage, and with Legge the less congenial duty of finding the money; Temple was replaced at the Admiralty by a great sea-officer, Anson, and made Lord Privy Seal; Granville (Carteret) continued as Lord President, and Hardwicke, without any office, retained his seat in the "efficient Cabinet." No less significant was Henry Fox's acceptance of Pitt's former post as Paymaster-General. Apparently he had definitely ended by his own act a political career; a peerage, and a fortune built up out of the Paymaster's "lawful perquisites," in the most expensive of wars so far, were now his avowed ambition, and in the fortune that his cool head and financial insight piled up he was only equalled, but not surpassed, by a later and even more unscrupulous Paymaster, Rigby. But if Fox, in 1757, deliberately walked off the political stage, he was able to show five years later that he had neither forgiven nor forgotten his "treatment" in 1756 and 1757.

In July 1757 the situation was worse than it had been six or twelve months ago. In North America the French held all the strategic points. After the capture of Oswego, with its flotilla, the entrance to the St. Lawrence was protected by the key-base at Louisburg which Loudon and Holbourne had failed to take; Frederick's preventive campaign had not gone as he had planned, and a sanguinary defeat at Kolin (June 18th) followed by Cumberland's defeat and convention of Klosterzeven (July 26th), preceded by the loss of Fort William (Calcutta) and the famous-infamous tragedy of "the Black Hole" and of Fort St. David, increased the public depression. Nor did Pitt help himself by his effort to save Byng (shot, March 14th) or, in the autumn, his political enemy, Cumberland, from the anger of his father, who now saw his beloved Hanover defenceless against Richelieu, the conqueror of Minorca. But, although it could not realise it, the Great Britain of the summer of 1757 stood on the threshold of an immortal chapter in its history. To the men and women with reverse and defeat following on reverse and defeat the position in 1761 would have seemed an incredible miracle; to the men and women of 1761 the situation in 1756 and 1757 had passed into a nightmare which they had already forgotten.

In January 1757 Pitt had taken 10, St. James's Square (now Chatham House), to be near his office in Cleveland Row, which was henceforth the General Headquarters of the war. His first four months of power had not been wasted and plans made then were coming slowly into execution, even during the interregnum. And he now took them up with demoniac energy. Pitt, like Nelson, never trifled with time, tide or wind. The "system" and the "decision" which he demanded in opposition were hammered, line upon line, precept upon precept, into a unified strategic scheme and control.

The situation was critical, not merely because a half-armed empire was quite unprepared for war, as is usual in our history, but because the Newcastle government, though the war had been seen coming for at least three years, could not make up its mind either as to principles or objectives; it was like Coleridge on Highgate Hill, who started to walk down one path and then down another and never for all his walking reached the bottom of the garden. Was it to be mainly a land war, or mainly a sea war, or in some indetermined proportion a combination? So far they had simply tried to hit back or defend, at any point, where the enemy had struck—sheer insanity or futility with a vulnerability wide-flung over two hemispheres and with inferior resources in man-power and material.

How the few men in our history standing out as masters of war learned their business remains still a mystery. The great Elizabethan seamen understood war, as did Cromwell and the Protectorate and Marlborough and the Whigs of 1702 to 1710; Chatham is in the small first division of the first class though he failed to transmit the gift to his son, William; and from the moment that "decision" or power came into his hands stamped his measures with "the Chatham touch."

Underlying what was done on sea and land, the Secretary of State in Cleveland Row saw the imperial problem with fundamental principles and objectives in his mind. The Empire was an expanding, loosely knit organisation with trade as its main purpose; dominions not dominion were its life-blood; stations from and to which the essentials of trade could freely flow were the links, which might become chains binding the English race, with its English "interest" and "way of life," a self-governing organic life united by allegiance to a single sovereign repeating across sundering seas the quality of purpose that had made a small island the motherland and the fruitful parent of many Englands to be. It was in the inscrutable scheme of Providence that this should be so, for Chatham shared with Cromwell and Milton an intense conviction that the English were the instruments (not the sole instruments) of a Divine Mission:

> Time and the Ocean and some fostering Star,
> In high cabal have made us what we are.

This racial and trading organisation had one principal foe and rival—France (behind which lurked the sinister league of a Bourbon Family Compact—Spain and Naples), and France stood for everything fatal to our empire, in race, religion, system of government and trade supremacy. France must, therefore, be made impotent, and until she "was laid upon her back" our empire could neither be safe nor grow: it would shrivel into a small island, living on sufferance and poor. Accordingly, in this war we fought "as much as merchants as soldiers."

Secondly, Pitt, without saying so explicitly, had grasped the fundamental truth that in war, if your strategy is sound, you can afford, and recover from, tactical mistakes, however regrettable in themselves; but that if your strategy is unsound, even tactical successes will not bring you to victory. And in

1756–7 a sound strategy clearly indicated that victory could only be won by the selection of the right area, and the concentration in and on it of superior force: all other areas would be ex-centric, subordinated both in ends and means, a defensive relative to the major offensive. This was all the more necessary for Great Britain whose war potential was in the nature of things inferior to the French potential.

Command of the sea was the unifying force and the base lay in Great Britain, that "water-walled bulwark, hedged in with the main," and supremacy in the home waters meant not only security from invasion but power to strike at any point selected overseas; there would be safety for a sea-borne trade from and to all the trading stations, big or little, near or far, and, as a consequence, denial of striking power from a home base and of trade in or out to the enemy. Wealth would tell and could only come from trade; and, as in 1702–1711, to use the phrase of Louis XIV, it would be the last *louis d'or*—and the last ship—that would win, and Great Britain must, and therefore could, have them.

When we speak, therefore, of Pitt's "system" we mean two separate but co-ordinated things—the principles of his strategy and the machinery and methods by which the principles were carried out. As regards the latter, Pitt simply used the existing organs and institutions. He revived through the inner cabinet the Supreme War Council so effectively operative between 1702 and 1711 by the Whigs—a fluid body of the half-dozen political or administrative heads, to which anyone could be summoned whose judgment or knowledge would be helpful for a particular problem or issue. Decisions, approved by the Crown, became orders through the appropriate officer, particularly the Secretaries of State. If desirable, a full Cabinet could be summoned, but the inner "conciliabulum" was the mainspring and a real War Cabinet. If nine plans out of ten were Pitt's, he was not a "sole minister"; the King's consent must be obtained and a unanimous advice provided the necessary pressure, while Newcastle, as nominal Prime Minister, was a more agreeable channel of communication than Pitt to a sovereign retaining to the end his distrust and personal dislike for a man "who will not do my business."

Patronage and its complicated relations to both Houses of Parliament was left to Newcastle. "Persuasion" by argument was Pitt's task, and for three years few if any in the Lower House dared articulate dissent. The voice and gesture of a Garrick and that terrible eye, with such a sentence as—"If there is an Austrian among you, let him stand forth"—sufficed. Murray, now in the House of Lords, professed absorption in the law, and Henry Fox, watching the rise and fall of the Funds, kept his thoughts to paper or stored up in a cold-blooded heart for a day that might come.

The application of a sound strategy, translated into officers, men, ships and equipment, was a continuous and Protean problem. Once Pitt had decided that North America and French Canada in particular was the strategic area for a concentrated superiority of force, the tactical plan had to be settled. It came to be a triple offensive—the capture of Louisburg, leading to an advance by sea up an ice-free St. Lawrence to Quebec and Montreal (which could only be between May and September)—a land offensive from New York via the Hudson River, Ticonderoga and Lake Champlain cutting the St. Lawrence between Quebec and Montreal, and a flanking movement from Lake Ontario and down the St. Lawrence eastwards to meet the advance via Lake Champlain. The West Indies were the outer sphere of the strategic area and an essential part of it, the eastern rim of which touched the west coast of Africa.

Military and trade necessities combined to unify the plan, for the lines of communication would be secure if the essential bases at either end were in British hands. And of these bases Great Britain was the key and nodal centre—at Chatham, Portsmouth and Plymouth. Lock up Dunkirk, Cherbourg, Brest and Rochefort—cut by Gibraltar the connection between Toulon and the western French sea-board, and not only would invasion be reduced to "landing by evasion," but the French would be unable to operate effectively either on the St. Lawrence or in the West Indies.

Against invasion by evasion Pitt anticipated the view of the St. Vincent-Nelson age; it could only be a nuisance raid, to be dealt with by the home troops. The enemy's battle fleet must either be defeated at sea or bottled up in separated squadrons at harbours isolated from each other, and then the protection of "the trade" could be provided by the light forces. A *guerre de course* by the enemy was a confession of weakness, no doubt annoying to "the City" and "the moneyed interest," but unable to affect the major strategy and the objectives of a sea-power rightly using its geographical advantages on the interior lines. Pitt, in 1758, '59 and '60 when Choiseul, whose abilities he rightly respected, replaced the mediocre Bernis and took up Belleisle's project of a blow at the heart by invasion across the Channel, refused to be rattled or to divert to home defence a single man allocated for the major offensive overseas. The battle-fleet would deal with the enemy battle-fleet; and a raid would recoil on the raiders. In a word, as Granville had once put it: "The sea when covered (i.e. commanded) is our defence, when not so covered it is our prison." If the ministry from 1774 onwards had only mastered the lesson Pitt now taught the nation, how different might have been North's Seven Years War. But a complacent mediocrity is as unwilling as it is unable to learn the lessons of genius, or of common sense.

The land war was a difficult problem. Pitt very soon shed his "juvenile errors" and grasped the necessity of taking some part in the war on the Continent, not merely to protect Hanover, "the King's business," but essential to our one ally, Prussia, for the Dutch, to whom neither Frederick nor North America meant anything, were obstinate in their churlish neutrality. "Containing operations" are a technical term very difficult to define beyond emphasis on the obvious principle of a defensive in a secondary strategic area subordinated to a concentrated offensive in the major strategic field. For Pitt they had a triple justification: Hanover could best be "saved" by "saving" Frederick, for what availed it to conquer Canada if the French established their supremacy in north and central Germany? When peace came to be made it would be, as in 1748, the exchange of Louisburg and the St. Lawrence basin for the equivalent losses in Europe or elsewhere; the credit and debit would simply cancel out. A force on the Weser would divert large French forces from being used against us across the Atlantic; and France must face the dilemma of deciding whether the most vital French "interest" lay in north-west Germany or on the St. Lawrence and in the West Indies.

If for Pitt the danger of "containing operations" was that they would grow into a competing major offensive, the French failed to solve the dilemma imposed on them by geography and tradition. France was a great power with a land frontier that made the Rhine a natural boundary to the East but with a sea frontier, also, both on the Atlantic and the Mediterranean, where the nature of sea-power sums up and provides the solution of the problem of France outside Europe. And the French with all their logical genius for clear thinking have at various epochs in their history only solved the dilemma, either because they were not at war with a sea-power or were in alliance with a sea-power which relieved them of the difficulty. Pitt, therefore, had no difficulty in convincing both himself and the ministerialists that the increasing share in "the land war" was a "true English interest" and had the support of "the Tories," his most enthusiastic supporters, "confident that the money (so lavishly voted), though some of it should go into Germany, will ever be employed to British purposes only." But his claim that "Canada had been won in Germany" was (and he knew it) simply an orator's deceptive rhetoric. Six Mindens could not have taken Quebec, for behind Wolfe and Saunders was the command of the sea. The glittering phrase had just as much or as little truth as the phrase, not so well known, that "success had given us unanimity and not unanimity success."

The continuous raids on the French coast (plausibly described by Henry Fox as "breaking windows with guineas") were not really "containing operations." For Pitt they were a subsidiary complement to the major operations for the "command of the sea"; they pinned down enemy men, ships and material, and not merely at the points attacked; they were a corrosive acid on bases from which an invasion might be launched, proving that the initiative was in our hands. If they were not as successful as they ought to have been, it was due to lack of experience in "amphibious operations," requiring complete co-operation between Navy and Army and especially to very inferior commanders of the troops forced upon him by the Crown. Frederick, who knew more of war than Henry Fox and the loungers at White's Club, testified to their military value and clamoured for more of such windows to be broken. Nor must we forget that Pitt was always thinking ahead to peace, and he wanted to have in his hand a good card, that he could discard safely to get back Minorca and not have to sacrifice one of his aces from a major suit. Belle-Isle was to be such a card. It was also a mustard-plaster on a very sensitive part of the French anatomy.

In these respects Pitt showed his comprehensive grasp as a master of war. Realising as he did that in man-power Great Britain was very inferior to the French (a point never to be forgotten in our eighteenth-century wars and making allies an absolute necessity), he exploited to the full our potential, which was as much financial as human. With a population of perhaps, at a maximum, eight millions against a French minimum of probably twenty millions he could get 100,000 for the Army and seventy thousand for the Navy—and he got them. By 1761 he had approximately 115 regiments up to strength as compared with 49 depleted regiments in 1748, and he utilised the fighting capacity of the Scottish Highlands by raising Scottish battalions, who "conquered for you in every part of the world" and inaugurated the tradition of several famous units in the century to follow. His political independence could justly claim: "I sought for merit wherever it was to be found." In addition, he reintroduced his Militia Bill, rejected in the Lords before he took office, and, though Mansfield and others mutilated it, in its amended form it provided some thirty to forty thousand for home defence and freed the army proper from that secondary job.

Financially, the war budget leaped up from four to nineteen millions and the national debt was doubled, rising from 72 to 147 millions. No wonder that Newcastle voiced the heart-cry of many when he half-sobbed out: "I wish to God I could see my way through this mountain of expense." But in 1763 Great Britain was not like France, really bankrupt. The "torrent" of expenditure had brought solid dividends (as well as victory). British internal and sea-borne trade and the merchant marine were larger in 1762 than in 1755, while French sea-borne trade and marine had sunk almost to zero.

Secondly, Pitt utilised the surplus in the New, partly to make good the deficiency in the Old, World. Until his day the Britain overseas had never been brought properly into an imperial war. The thirteen colonies with a population probably of at least a million and a half (as against 100,000 French at a maximum in Canada) were very soon taught that in London was a minister who meant to do "their business," and who intuitively understood what was in their English and colonial hearts. And Pitt succeeded in making thirteen jealous and refractory legislatures and their electors combine as they had never combined before in an imperial war for an imperial issue. The published volumes of his colonial despatches show how he did it, as appeals, orders, instructions flowed out from Cleveland Row, backed by the demonstrable reality of the British Navy and battalion after battalion arriving from the Motherland.

And in some inexplicable way the flame of inspiration in 10, St. James's Square leaped the Atlantic to kindle fires, smouldering at best in the gloom of depression and distrust. Spirit can speak to spirit across sundering seas without material connection: Pitt's phrase in a later and unhappy day—"You can only grasp America in the arms of affection"—reveals the secret. The Empire for him was a deeper and greater unity than a prosperous trading organisation; its essence and its strength were spiritual, not material, and wherever the flag flew it stood for spiritual realities expressed in an English way of life, born of the spirit in the travail of the centuries. Pitt, therefore, came to be a man and an inspiring power for millions of men and women who never saw his face or heard his voice, and the tangible proof is in the three statues (at Dedham, Mass.; New York and Charleston) and in the renaming of Fort Duquesne as Fort Pitt (the modern Pittsburgh of Carnegie fame).

Thirdly, Pitt's campaigns were based not only on untiring pains over details but on the most accurate information he could get. A well-organised Secret Service and the interception of letters and despatches were supplemented by what he could learn either from the men on the spot or the traders who knew the value of this or that station, as a source of raw materials or as the key point of a distributive commerce. He did not have to learn, as Horace Walpole would have us believe Newcastle did, that Cape Breton was an island and why Annapolis (to be found after inquiry on the map) must be defended. From Governor Pownall and the like, from "the fighting Quaker" Cumming and other friends in "the City," from the headquarters of the East India Company or the Royal African Company, Pitt sought the information that might make for success or failure.

India was strictly "ex-centric," a field of rivalry between two chartered and trading corporations rather than a duel between London and Versailles, but so far as he could Pitt gave in ships, men and munitions the material and moral aid which, in the crisis of its destinies in the East, France to our astonishment denied to its servants. Our records at least are not stained with the treatment meted out to Dupleix, Lally and Bussy. To Clive and Eyre Coote Pitt could pay the tribute by which genius enhances its own worth.

But analyse as fully and scientifically as we may Pitt's principles and measures, there remains an unanalysable force —the man himself. England, the British Empire and their foes realised after December 1756 that something unpredictable and undefinable had happened, and that there was a new wind blowing—whence and whither who could say?— which filled the lungs of weary men and made them feel greater than they had ever dreamed. "One spirit's plastic stress sweeps through the dull sense world," and, as Ezekiel saw in the valley of dry bones, the breath came into them and they lived and stood upon their feet. It was truly said that no man talked with Pitt but went out braver than he came in. "You," said Pitt to Boscawen, "find expedients when others find excuses." Those were the men he wanted and found—in time. And if, when we speak of Pitt as a War Minister, we do not put the quality of his spirit first, we have missed the secret of the man and his achievement.

No less inexplicable is the physical fact that for the four and a half years from June 1757 to October 1761 Pitt, who probably in the whole course of his life never enjoyed twelve months of normal health, bore the terrible strain of work and responsibility without one crippling breakdown. Hester Grenville almost certainly contributed to this mysterious result, and Pitt may later have paid a cruel price for the strain endured so triumphantly, for he was to learn that he could only do it once, to the incalculable loss of Great Britain and the Empire.

In all wars the right measures by the best brains never work out exactly according to plan. Apart from the "fog"— the difficulty of divining what "the man on the other side of the hill" intends to do—all the greater in an age which had neither steam, electricity, wireless nor aeroplanes, when ships could be the victims of "foul" weather for weeks and gales blew from wrong quarters, and when pathology was scarcely in its cradle, allowance has always to be made for "luck," for lapses in human minds (such as in peace or civil life cause important letters not to be posted and railway accidents to occur, because a signalman "forgot") and to an unsuspected incapacity, only revealed when an individual unexpectedly "fails" in a critical situation, or to the chance, if it be so, when the best are killed and the mediocre come through scatheless. If Durell in the spring of 1758 had been (as was intended) a week earlier in the ice-floes off the mouth of the St. Lawrence, he would have sunk the French squadron, not only bringing reinforcement to Quebec but an intercepted letter, revealing the plan of campaign, and Wolfe and Boscawen after Louisburg would probably have taken Quebec by surprise that year.

Pitt's "raids" on the French coast suffered much from the King's determination to keep as his prerogative the royal right to "command," and George, an old man, believed in seniority and his own poor judgment, in spite of the lesson taught him by Cumberland; Mordaunt, Marlborough, Bligh, forced on Pitt, were as responsible for failures as was Pitt's eldest son ("the late Lord Chatham") responsible for Walcheren in 1809. Could Abercromby, Loudon and Holbourne in North America have been substituted as casualties for the loss of the gallant and capable Forbes and Howe, success and not failure would have been on the record of that year. Lord George Sackville's extraordinary refusal twice to obey his orders at Minden prevented Ferdinand and Granby from inflicting a crushing defeat. Unhappily a court martial and dismissal did not prevent Lord George from doing much worse mischief, under his patron, George III, later on; and only a British Dante in an eighteenth-century "Inferno" would have found the right circle for his baleful life.

The list might easily be extended. Nor in an audited balance-sheet can the credits, incarnated in Clive, Eyre Coote and Wolfe, in Saunders, Hawke and Boscawen—a naval trio who opened a new chapter leading through Rodney and the Hoods to the classical age of St. Vincent and Nelson—be accurately estimated against the debits.

Pitt was really sole foreign minister, for Holdernesse was a cowed colleague who did what his dominating brother Secretary required; and apart from the other members of the War Cabinet who growled and sulked there were the neutrals and our ally, Prussia, to manage. In every one of our big wars command of the sea and blockades have inevitably exasperated neutrals, whose "rights" conflict with a sea-power's definition of contraband and the claim to "search," as against the transfer of goods, including enemy goods, to protection under a neutral flag. And in the eighteenth century the whole "law of privateering," easily degenerating on both sides into pure piracy, complicated a problem which was really one of policy rather than of law. Pitt, pressed by powerful British trading interests clamouring for every sea, and particularly the Atlantic and the Mediterranean, to be made "safe," and by all the maritime neutrals from the Baltic to the Barbary Pirates clamouring for "the freedom of the seas," was determined above all to keep Spain and the kindred Bourbon dynasty in Naples out of the war; he had also to placate the Dutch, who ought to have been our belligerent allies, and the Baltic States, an indispensable source of raw material for our Navy. And when Spain did "come in," the violation of "neutral rights" was not the real cause.

Pitt discovered, also, as has every ministry before and since his time, that even a doubled navy would not be large enough to do the job that everyone asked of it. Ships without trained sailors are as useless as dynamos without engineers, and we ought rather to admire the solid results rather than criticise the obvious deficiencies in the amazing effort of a small island with a population of only eight millions, operating in every sea.

Allies are difficult in every age, because the community of interest uniting any two states is never so strong as the diversity which pulls them apart. And Frederick of Prussia was no exception. We were fortunate no doubt in an ally personified in a genius, inexhaustible in his energy and industry, who recognised similar qualities in Pitt. But for Frederick the war had but one object, to save Prussia, and in the interest of Prussia he would have evicted his mother as easily as he parted company with his unhappy queen. It was the privilege and duty of Great Britain to "work for Prussia." "I laugh at the friendship of England," he wrote in 1760, "if it is no use to me," and he would have backed out of the Convention of Westminster, with its subsidy doubled in 1758, if the integrity of Prussia could have been gained thereby. A sacred egoism to be really effective requires that every other state will act on the principles of the Ten Commandments and the Sermon on the Mount, while it also assumes that your neighbour has no moral right to treat you as you will treat him, if reason of state clearly indicates that that is your interest.

What Pitt had, as a fact, to face was that, with a population of five and a half millions, Prussia with Russia to the east, the Austrians to the south and the French to the west, he was tackling a job beyond his powers, even if he had the advantage of the interior lines. Genius, up to a certain limit, can make good an inferiority in man-power, but even within that limit genius requires troops of the same quality as itself. Napoleon in 1814, Lee in Virginia in 1864, were to exemplify what Frederick's war reveals by 1760. Diminishing quality and numbers as against increasing quality and numbers can only end one way. And the same plain moral stands out in the basin of the St. Lawrence in 1759 and 1760, where the English had better leaders and superiority in numbers: for Nelson's axiom that "numbers alone can annihilate" is as true of the land as of the sea. Pitt saw that if Prussia succumbed, Hanover would be lost, for a proclamation of neutrality by the Electorate would be laughed at by the victorious confederacy. For him, and then for Great Britain, the real problem was how long could Frederick last, by how much could we safely increase our effort on the Ems and the Weser and how much more of defeat outside Europe would France stand? and this problem was to be complicated by two deaths and two accessions—George III to his grandfather's throne, and Charles III to that of Ferdinand in Spain, neither of which of necessity had to happen when they did.

The first phase of the war, therefore, ends with the death of George II. And as military history can only be profitably studied in detail, a bare summary must suffice, which can be filled in according to a reader's need or taste.[2]

---

[2] E.g. in standard works (with their bibliographies) such as the biographies by Carlyle (6 vols. to 1763), B. Williams and B. Tunstall; J. Corbett, *England in the Seven Years War* (2 vols. mainly naval); J. W. Fortescue, *History of the British Army;* and (in French) R. Waddington, *La Guerre de Sept Ans* (5 vols.).

In July 1757 the situation was depressing: for the failures at Rochefort and Louisburg and the loss of Fort William Henry, a drawn battle against the Russians at Gross-Jägersdorf and Cumberland's capitulation at Hastenbeck, had made both the British and Frederick's situation very serious, but it was saved in November by the two classic victories in the West and East at Rosbach and Leuthen. In 1758 the sun of victory began to emerge above the horizon. Thanks to Boscawen and Wolfe, Louisburg and Cape Breton Island were taken—which caused more rejoicing on both sides of the Atlantic than any other successes in the war—and naval victories off Carthagena and the Basque Roads checked the counter-offensive of an invasion, planned by Choiseul. A new subsidy Treaty, raising the amount to £670,000, and the replacement of the mediocre Cumberland by the competent Ferdinand of Brunswick, reinforced from Great Britain, gave the King of Prussia, finding the Russians the most stubborn of his foes, substantial aid on his western flank.

The way was open, with the capture of Goree (December) in West Africa, to the "year of Victory," 1759. Overseas, Guadeloupe was taken; Wolfe, with the indispensable help of a great sea-officer, Saunders, after four months of probing and trial by error, found the cove that now bears his name, and on the heights and plain above won the battle that cost him his life and gained Quebec (September 13–18th). In Europe, Prince Ferdinand's victory at Minden (July 1st), which, but for Lord George Sackville's refusal to obey orders, would have been crushing, was the suitable prelude to the naval victories of Boscawen and Hawke. True to type, Fighting Black Dick ignored "the rights of neutrals" at Lagos, as Hawke (November 20th–21st) ignored the darkness and gale at Quiberon while the combined blows, "coming to us as from the Lord," mortally wounded the French battle-fleet. It was not, however, a good year for Frederick; Kunersdorf and Maxen inflicted irreparable losses on his diminishing forces, and he was only saved by winter and "the divine stupidity of his enemies."

In 1760 Pitt's chief anxiety was "how long could Frederick

continue," even if Prince Ferdinand were reinforced, as he was. Pomerania was in Swedish hands, the Russians were in the New Mark and had raided Berlin, while Silesia was occupied by the Austrians. And Frederick's plight was not relieved by the fall of Montreal to the triple converging movement from the south, east and west. New France (Canada) and the St. Lawrence basin were now in British hands. It was the same story in India. When Clive returned to England in this year he could report that by his victory at Plassey (1757) and his vigorous action in the valley of the Ganges not only was Calcutta safe but the British were supreme in Bengal up to the southern frontier of Oudh, and that the military and political power of French and Dutch had gone for ever. In the Carnatic, Eyre Coote's victory at Wandiwash (January 1761) and the fall of Pondicherry "sounded the knell of French dominion in India." In fact, two great problems in imperial policy had now to be faced: what was to be done with Canada? was the Crown to take the place of the East India Company in the huge peninsula of Hindustan? The solution must inevitably raise in a new form the future of the British Empire in two hemispheres; and there were no precedents to shape the decision.

During the year 1760, the war in fact had changed its character. Starting as a war with a limited objective—the Anglo-French issue in North America—it had become, as big wars always do, a war with unlimited objectives; and this was clearly grasped by Choiseul, who, since 1758, controlled the war effort and diplomacy of France. The anti-British Charles of "The Two Sicilies" had, as Charles III, succeeded to the friendly Ferdinand VI as ruler of the "neutral" Spanish Empire. Choiseul had in his drawer at the Quai D'Orsay what he thought would be a trump card—the Family Compacts of 1733 and 1743, which could now be renewed at Madrid; and, if Pitt would not agree to a reasonable peace, Spain would be brought into the war and recover for the Bourbon coalition the command of the Atlantic and Mediterranean. Death seemed to be on the side of Choiseul, for on October 26th a galloping groom brought to Prince George, on his way to Kew, the unexpected news that his grandfather had been found dead that morning in his closet. The King at St. James's Palace was dead. Long live the new King at Leicester House. Well might the stricken Newcastle write: "God knows what consequences the King's death may have."

Death was not wholly on Choiseul's side. On January 19th, 1762, the Tsarina Elizabeth was the first of the *trois catins* to go; the second, the Pompadour, survived until 1764 for her last cold and wet journey in her coffin from Versailles, and the third, at Vienna, kept her son, Joseph, from effective rule until 1780; to Elizabeth succeeded a half-mad Tsar, Peter, a fanatical admirer of the King of Prussia, "a divine man," as Frederick wrote, "to whom I ought to erect altars," for Tsar Peter promptly withdrew from the eastern frontier of Prussia the most stubborn and ferocious of its foes. Frederick could now, with his undefeated brother, Henry, recover Silesia from the Austrian grip.

"Dapplings for peace" had begun in London; and in 1760 the resounding success of a pamphlet, *Considerations on the Present German War*, proved that victory had wrought a great change in public opinion. The author, Israel Mauduit, of Huguenot origin, was a rich woollen draper who argued with marked ability two main points: England was wasting blood and treasure in a land war, solely in the interest of Hanover and Prussia; she had won at sea and could obtain a decisive peace by concentrating wholly on the sea war. Mauduit, in fact, achieved almost as great a success as Swift, half a century earlier, had in his *Conduct of the Allies*. For he expressed explicitly, as Swift had done in 1710, the question that "the political nation" was now asking—why go on fighting for selfish allies when we can get from France everything that an English interest can reasonably demand? What are Silesia or Hanover to us, when we can exchange the capture of Belle-Isle for Minorca and retain what we need in North America, the West Indies, Coromandel and Bengal?

Mauduit was an unforeseen ally to Leicester House, which wanted peace for very different reasons and realised that the obstacle to peace was incarnate in one man—Pitt. "I would rather go and row in the galleys," observed Choiseul, "than have to discuss any kind of peace with Mr. Pitt." For Pitt made it clear that he would make peace only on two conditions: Frederick must not be "deserted," and both Prussia (with Silesia) and Hanover must remain intact for their lawful rulers; France must not be left in North America with dangerous footholds such as the bases of her fishing fleet at St. Pierre and Miquelon, off Newfoundland. But as the negotiations flowed from Paris to London and back again Pitt suspected that Choiseul was determined to bring Spain into the business. And matters came to a head. Pitt had learned of the renewed Family Compact (August 15th) and guessed, though he could not prove, that Spain had agreed to become a belligerent, if "satisfactory" terms had not been settled by the end of the year, which would thus enable the Treasure fleet to reach Vigo and Cadiz safely before entering the war as an ally of France. On the sound principle not to allow an enemy to declare war when it suited him, Pitt, therefore, demanded an ultimatum which would either bring Spain into the war before the Treasure fleet had safely crossed the Atlantic or compel Choiseul to make peace without Spain as an ally. The Cabinet was against this drastic action, partly because the aged Anson and Ligonier, the naval and military experts, pronounced that we were not ready to add a formidable foe to our commitments, partly because the majority were not convinced that Pitt's diagnosis of Choiseul's plans was correct, and partly because the young King and Bute wished either to get rid of Pitt or to make it clear that policy and peace were in their and not his hands. Supported only by Temple, Pitt's ultimatum was rejected, and he and Temple promptly resigned. "The Great Ministry" had ended. (October 5th, 1761.)[3]

[3] It is now agreed that the speech of Earl Granville, reported in *The Annual Register,* in which he emphasised that in Cabinet the members were responsible only to the King and not to the House of Commons, is not authentic and was probably the work of Burke, the editor, who misinterpreted an inaccurate account of what Granville really said.

Events soon showed that Pitt had been right. Once the Treasure fleet had reached Spain, Grimaldi, the Spanish ambassador to France, came into the open, and our Cabinet without Pitt found itself at war (January 2nd, 1762) exactly as he had predicted. Fortunately the measures planned by Pitt could be put into operation, and the capture of Havana "cut Grimaldi's cackle" as effectively as a frost in May can devastate a year's fruit crop. It had been preceded by the capture of Martinique, St. Lucia and Grenada, and was followed by the capture of Manila and the collapse of a renewed plan of invasion by the fertile Choiseul. "The Family Compact" was proving a disaster to both Bourbon allies; but the victories were an embarrassing nuisance to the peacemakers in London.

The King and Bute were determined for their own reasons to make peace, at any price; Newcastle was forced out of office (May 25th); and the now pacifist and Little Englander, Bedford, was sent to Paris with imperative instructions, so that the Preliminaries were signed on November 3rd, 1762. It only remained to force them through Parliament. To Fox was assigned the congenial task of completing the "rout of the Whigs," and so efficiently did he work that, despite Pitt's opposition in a speech of more than three hours, the Preliminaries were approved in the Lords, without a division, and in the Commons by 319 to 65 votes. The Preliminaries became the Treaty of Paris (February 10th, 1763) between Great Britain, France and Spain and the basis of the Treaty of Hubertusburg between Prussia and the House of Austria (February 15th). The Seven Years War had ended.

Great Britain secured Canada, Senegal, St. Vincent, Tobago and the Grenadines, the return of Minorca, the restriction of France in India to factories established before 1749, and Florida (from Spain, which received Louisiana in compensation from France); but she returned (without compensation) Manila, Havana, Martinique, and St. Lucia and Goree, and the St. Lawrence and Newfoundland fisheries, together with Miquelon and St. Pierre—rights which perpetuated serious friction until they were finally extinguished in 1904. Freder-

ick was not in the end "betrayed," though he remained convinced of England's "treachery," for, thanks to Halifax, at
the last moment he recovered all the territory he had lost
and Silesia with the county of Glatz was confirmed as a
Prussian province.

On his deathbed Granville thought the terms "the most
honourable peace," ending "the most glorious war this nation ever saw," but to Pitt they were "wholly inadmissible";
we had treated Frederick basely, after profiting by his victories and costly sacrifice; we had failed to destroy the
strength of France "as a maritime and commercial power";
we had surrendered decisive conquests without adequate
compensation, and, worst of all, we had "given to France
the means of recovering her prodigious losses and of
becoming once more formidable to us at sea." In a word,
France and the Bourbon dynasties could now work for another war of revenge, the seeds of which were sown in the
Treaty.

Pitt's criticisms (to which there was no real answer) are
important because they confirm his principles of imperial
policy. The British Empire had fought successfully to maintain itself as a great trading and commercial organisation,
embodying the English interpretation of life, and resting on
the command of the sea and the bases necessary for that
command; it had also found in Frederick an ally, Protestant
and tolerant, as an effective counter-poise to the Catholic,
absolutist and intolerant combination of Paris, Madrid and
Vienna. Prussia had taken the place of the waning and peevish Dutch; and to Prussia Russia, by the right diplomacy on
our part, might now be added, checkmating a Bourbon-Habs-
burg domination of western and central Europe. For Pitt
never forgot that, if trade and commerce were our life-blood,
the British Empire was the only free Empire in the world—
a free Crown ruling over a free and self-governing people—
and a secret of our strength lay in its spiritual convictions
and constitutional government. The next fifteen years were
to show how deep these principles were embedded in his
statesmanship and personality.

But despite their glaring defects, the Treaties registered two fundamental facts which moulded the future of the world: the British Empire, threatened with defeat and dissolution in 1756, had won a resounding victory, because it was now clear that North America was to be "English," while in Hindustan the only possible successor to the Mogul Empire, with its capital at Delhi, was Great Britain: no less momentous, Prussia had also survived the menace of partition and dismemberment, and, for good or evil, as a system of government and a political power, had come to stay. The immediate influence of Frederick and of Frederician Prussianism was to reach its zenith in the next twenty years— and to survive the French Revolution. Never was it truer for our country and for Europe that a great war if it ends one epoch always opens another.

PART TWO
1760-1778

1. 1760–1763: Lord Bute and The Peace

IT IS GENERALLY AGREED that the accession of George III on
October 26th, 1760, opened a new epoch in British history,
and until some years ago it was held (and stated in the text-
books, big and small) that the main and formative feature
of this new epoch was the deliberate and determined plan
of the new King and his chief adviser, Bute, to "recover"
the lost prerogatives of the monarchy, to destroy the "constitutional" system of party government, through the Crown
in Parliament, established by the Whigs in the two preceding
reigns, to set back the clock in the fundamental principles of
administration, and to inaugurate, with the organised system
of Janissaries known as "The King's Friends," a regime of
personal rule by the sovereign, on the lines of Bolingbroke's
Idea of a Patriot King, in which the Crown resumed its right
to govern with ministers freed from all party creeds or
allegiances and responsible only to a Crown, above all parties,
the extinction of which was its duty. It was taken for granted
that Bolingbroke's little treatise (published in 1749) was the
text-book on which Leicester House and the Dowager Princess of Wales, with the subsequent aid of Lord Bute, brought
up the heir to the throne, after the unfortunate death of
Frederick Prince of Wales, with the repeated maxim,
"George, be a King." This system of a restored personal
monarchy was held to have been exposed by Burke in his

Thoughts on the Causes of the Present Discontent (1770), which became the classical statement of the true constitutional system and principles alike of cabinet, parliamentary and party government, and an unanswerable indictment of the "revolutionary reaction" begun by Bute and culminating in the ministry of Lord North (1770), until it crashed in the American War of Independence, when a return to the right system was made by the younger Pitt in 1784. On this view the struggle with the American colonies simply exemplified the same disastrous effort to set up personal and "absolute" government across the Atlantic through a docile legislature at Westminster, as was being carried out in the motherland.

Modern research[1] in the last fifteen years has completely disposed of this orthodox interpretation, for it has shown that it rested upon a misunderstanding of what the system from 1715 to 1760 really was; that Burke's famous treatise was not an accurate analysis of what George III found in existence on his accession, and set about to destroy, but an idealised picture of what a cabinet and party government might be on certain assumptions which did not correspond either with the facts or with what the Rockingham or any group of Whigs did or would have done, had they been in office with adequate power during the first ten years of the new King's reign; and that nineteenth-century historians, misled by Burke, read into the eighteenth-century fabric of administration the principles of cabinet and party government as expounded by Bagehot in his *English Constitution* (1867) and not really worked out until the generation after the Reform Act of 1832.

The real novelty in 1760 was a combination of several elements not previously fused together—the personality and "education" of George III, the nature of his relations with Bute and the peculiar position created by his grandfather's death; for the young King, born in 1738, had by 1760 in-

[1] See particularly—Namier, *Structure of Politics on the Accession of George III* (2 vols. with the supplementary volume on the situation in 1768–1770) and Romney Sedgwick (with its Introduction), *The Letters of George III and Lord Bute.*

evitably inherited the traditional opposition of the heir to the throne, under the House of Hanover, to the reigning sovereign. Leicester House had been the centre of the "reversionary interest," strengthened in its antagonism by the obstinacy with which George II excluded his grandson from any and every share in the government which was bound to be his and could not be long postponed, and by his mother's seclusion of her son from the society of a Court and an aristocracy which she feared would corrupt his morals. Prince George, a backward youth of retarded development, grew up, therefore, ignorant of the social and political world of his day, and dependent for his views on life, politics, morals and conduct wholly on what he learned from his teacher and Groom of the Stole, Bute.

George II not unfairly said of the Tutor-Groom that he would have been an admirable minister of a German principality, where there was nothing to do. Handsome, for like Sir Willoughby Patterne he "had a leg," Bute had ambitions beyond his abilities and was handicapped by his ignorance of affairs and his Scottish blood, for neither Scottish peers nor Commoners had yet overcome the unpopularity of the "intruders" from the north, expressed so forcibly by men so different as Horace Walpole and Dr. Johnson. There is no evidence that Bute was inspired by Bolingbroke, whose treatise had fallen quite flat in 1749, or that the Princess Dowager of Wales was so infatuated by the Groom of the Stole that she and Bute aimed at repeating the parts played by Mortimer and Queen Isabella in 1327. What is quite certain is that Prince George was infatuated by Bute, that his views on everything, expressed in ungrammatical and misspelt English, were simply those put into his head by Bute, and that he grew up to regard his grandfather and St. James's Palace as the centre of a system manipulated by evil men for their own evil ends, and that it was his duty, when power came to him, to free the Crown from the bondage and fetters of the "faction" which had enslaved it, and that an upright and high-principled Groom of the Stole would be the main instrument to achieve this noble end. Bute, it has been well said, "panted for the Treasury and George III panted with him."

The idea of a patriotic King, freed from control of party (identified with mercenary faction), and choosing his ministers solely on their merits and to carry out the sovereign's disinterested policy, was not the creation of Bolingbroke, but had been a recognised formula in the political vocabulary for more than half a century; and it was an accepted axiom that when the "reversionary interest" came into its own, the existing ministerial "tyrants" would be dismissed in favour of a new and royal group, in turn to be opposed and then replaced by a "new reversionary interest." There was no such thing as "constitutional opposition"—an idea abhorrent to the eighteenth-century mind—there was only the legitimate object of the professedly uncorrupt out of office to eject the consciously corrupt in office, and so free the sovereign from the bondage of his bad advisers. Parties and party government, in short, as the nineteenth century came to understand them simply did not exist in 1760. The current remark of George Selwyn, the accepted wit of the day, that as there was nothing new under the sun, there was nothing new under the Grand-Son, was not true. The personality of the young King and the circumstances of 1760 caballed to make a wholly new situation.

The political and social world of St. James's, Mayfair and Westminster fully realised that the new King, in his twenty-second year, had been born in England, gloried in the name of "Briton" (or "Britain"), had never been at Herrenhausen, which, it was whispered at White's, he could not find on the map (and which in the course of a long life he never visited) and had not round him a camarilla of German bureaucrats or still hungrier German mistresses on the ground floor of the sovereign's headquarters with backdoors to the Royal Closet upstairs—here, indeed, Providence had provided a King to whom Tories, no less than Whigs, could do submissive homage. No less significant, and also for the first time since 1710, there was and could be no "reversionary interest," as Hardwicke emphatically stated. Get the King married at once, and as soon as Madam had done her duty and borne a Prince of Wales there could be no "reversionary interest" for at least a generation. Leicester House was now absorbed into St. James's Palace, and the only source of peerages, profit, patronage, pension or promissory notes was the Crown—with no rival in existence. The Bubb Dodingtons, the Rigbys, the Bloomsbury Gang, the careerists, aristocratic or parasitical, at once grasped this momentous fact; there was only one Sun now and the "factions" must turn to it—or wither at the roots. More than twenty years had to pass until once again, and true to type, a rebel Prince of Wales restarted at Carlton House "the reversionary interest" as a social and political force.

Such was the background which fate provided for Mr. Secretary Pitt in November 1760, wrestling with the war and doubly anxious as to what the new sovereign at Madrid might do, and whether the King of Prussia could last out another year. And at once a third anxiety was added. Every commitment inherited from his grandfather must be liquidated before the grandson, now King, could feel free from "the tyranny an old man groaned under." The war was not only "costly" and "bloody," but was a German war for "that horrid electorate which has always lived upon the very vitals of this poor country": Frederick of Prussia was a ruinous charge on the British Exchequer to be cut out as soon as possible; the ministers were evil men, the product of an evil age, to be replaced by untainted servants "as my (royal) tools solely in my public capacity"; peace was a crying necessity; the King of Prussia must be "forced into peace," and Pitt must be "forced out" of the Cabinet. For Mr. Secretary Pitt was the formidable obstacle to peace and a recovered freedom of action; he was the war, and so long as it continued he was indispensable, while his popularity, which exasperated both George III and Bute, would continue as he added victory to victory. But peace, they felt, was a better trump card than victory, and with it you could win trick, game and rubber.

George III lost no time. On October 27th, 1760, Bute was

sworn of the Privy Council, in March 1761 he succeeded Holdernesse as Secretary of State, in May he became a Scottish representative peer and so had his place in the House of Lords; on May 26th, 1762, the First Lordship of the Treasury, for which he "panted," was his, and next day he was a Knight of the Garter. He could rise no higher and the ministry was now his. Better still, Pitt had been forced to resign (October 5th, 1761), and his reputation discredited, for *The Gazette* in an unprecedented notice had carefully informed the public that His Majesty had conferred on Lady Hester Pitt a peerage as Baroness Chatham and on Pitt himself a pension of £3,000 a year for two further lives. The letters of Gray and Horace Walpole and the wail that surged up from the City confirmed the cynical shrugs and sneers of the clubs in St. James's Street; Pitt was after all of the same clay as everyone else and, as might be expected and was really quite natural, the "Great Commoner," so independent and incorruptible, had very sensibly taken his profit at the top of the market, and sold out "for a pension and a long-necked peeress," "Lady Cheat'em" as Grub Street now called her. Sejanus was down at last; there was now none so poor as to do him reverence or spare a kick or a jibe at the fallen Minister.

George III and Bute had played their game with great skill against a player, the veriest amateur in political intrigue and with a profound contempt for move and countermove in the chicanery of party manœuvres, and only formidable when imperial problems and the destiny of Great Britain were the absorbing issues at stake. Pitt had the arrogant Temple alone to support him in the Cabinet; he had offended the Duke of Bedford, the Lord-Lieutenant at Dublin and now the strongest of the group who wanted peace at any price; he had broken with Bute with whom he had been "connected" in 1759, and he had failed to see that he must either work with Newcastle or with Bute, while the King had come to regard him as, with the exception of Fox, the worst of his grandfather's ministers; nor did Pitt grasp the complete change in the mentality of the political nation, revealed by the success of Mauduit's pamphlet, still less that when New-castle, insulted, neglected and thwarted, was driven into resignation (May 1762), the whole governmental machine passed into the King and Bute's hands.

Pitt recovered rapidly, no doubt, from the unpopularity that his pension and the peerage for Lady Hester had created, and he was still the idol of public opinion, but Bute had driven a deep wedge between him and Newcastle, whom he regarded as a "traitor" in the settlement of the peace-terms, and he very soon learned (as others have done since) that cheers in the streets were not votes in the House of Commons. The only political organisation was the Treasury, and the King and Bute could take over intact the efficient machine, so laboriously controlled for thirty years by Newcastle. "If a lion knew his own strength," it was truly said of the Tudor monarchy under Henry VIII, "hard it were to rule him," and it was no less true of the Hanoverian Monarchy in 1760. It was not a question of revolution or reaction; all that George III had to do was, with an efficient minister as head of the Treasury, to make the sovereign the real director of the Treasury Tammany Hall and work the established system precisely as custom, convention and law had made it acceptable and intelligible to the political nation. The Crown could become, with hardly a stroke of the pen, what it was in theory, the source of honours, places, pensions, and control either its own, or drive a bargain with the private owners of, pocket boroughs.

In 1762 neither George III nor Bute had the necessary first-hand knowledge, though the young King was learning fast; a royal "Newcastle" must be found and he was at hand in Henry Fox, more than willing for a peerage and continuance at the lucrative Paymaster's office to "mak siccar" with the handful of Pittites and the larger group round Hardwicke and Newcastle. How efficiently and genially Fox could "go to the rout" and how strong was the Treasury machine was shown in both Houses of Parliament, for on the terms of Peace there was no division in the Upper, and in the Lower House only 65 votes, which included that of General

Clive, could be mustered against 319 for the administration. How were the mighty fallen! In 1759 scarcely a whisper against the Great Commoner; in 1762 scarcely a single member could be found to defend or support, and there were many to denounce or snarl at, the man, stricken with gout, who had won the war. "My son is now King." If the Dowager Princess of Wales did not say this, she could have said it with perfect truth.

And yet was he? The King had still to learn that in this peculiar free and parliamentary system the Crown could do everything with votes except sit upon them. Bute, the First Lord of the Treasury (May 26th, 1762), who had triumphantly carried his Peace Treaty and whose best act was the pension he secured for Dr. Johnson, resigned (April 8th, 1763), and Henry Fox, "the bad man" called in to "deal with bad men," refused to take his place. Bute, in fact, had got himself on to a slope in which he could neither go forward nor back; "The Thane, Sir Pertinax MacSycophant," was desperately unpopular, his relations with the Dowager Princess of Wales were matter for derisive and unsavoury libel, and the major problems of policy were beyond his capacity to handle. Terrified and disillusioned, he retired, only to find that as a "minister behind the curtain" he was even more detested than when he was in power. Cruellest of all, he was in 1765 abandoned by the King, who refused to see him; for by that date George III had convinced himself that he neither owed (nor had ever owed) anything to the "tutor" who had made his mind for what it was. With "my heart half-broke, my health ruined with the unmerited, barbarous treatment I have received," Bute slunk back into the obscurity from which he had emerged like a Painted Lady to flutter a brief summer in the caressing sunlight and then —the dark. Fox faded out at the same time. Disliked intensely by the King as an immoral politician, and as unpopular as Bute, he got the Barony (which, despite all his efforts, he failed to convert into an earldom) that he hungered for and was forced out of the Pay Office by the Rockingham Whigs. Did the old man, in the twilight of his days at Kingsgate in Kent, read Gray's bitter lampoon,[2] and consider that his Barony and his ill-gotten fortune were an adequate reward for the ability he had first shown under the great Walpole and that, if he could live his life over again, he would do exactly as he had done? We do not know; but at any rate Bute and he were the first, but not the last, to learn that gratitude was a virtue unknown to George III.

The King had set out to free the Crown from bondage and now, in 1763, discovered that, if the Whigs had been humiliated and broken, he had only been delivered back in still more galling fetters to "the Family," led by George Grenville, who after "boring his royal master for an hour looked at his watch to see how he could bore him for another hour." How to escape? There was one, and only one, man, the ex-Secretary, William Pitt, with his mystical reverence for the Crown, his rupture with his brothers-in-law, the Grenvilles of "the Family," and his avowed independence of all "parties" and "factions." Pitt was twice, if not thrice, approached and was willing to "come in"; but the first effort was ruined by Bute from "behind the curtain" and the second by Earl Temple, without whom Pitt refused to take office. The Rockingham Whigs were, with Newcastle, more than ready to line up behind him and accept his leadership, but Pitt, still sore over Whig "desertion" on the Peace, declined to put himself at their head, and "the Rockinghams" reluctantly replaced George Grenville under the patronage and pressure of the Duke of Cumberland, who died the same year. It was a lamentable decision on Pitt's part. In office in the summer of 1765 he could have formed a strong and liberal ministry (for the King was quite friendly) with the one man at its head in whom the country had complete confidence and under whose leadership the disasters and blunders of the next ten years might have been avoided. Temple was in no way indispensable; and on this occasion he was

[2] Old and abandoned by each venal friend,
   Here Holland found the pious resolution:
To smuggle a few years and strive to mend
   A broken character and constitution.

the *âme damnée* of his brother-in-law and the British Empire. For great issues had been raised in the two years after the Peace of 1763, requiring big and generous minds to solve them.

2. The Imperial and Domestic Problems: 1763–1765

The Peace of 1763 had reopened old and wholly new imperial problems of policy and administration. First and foremost there was North America stretching from the ill-defined territories of the Hudson Bay Company in the north to Florida, the mouth of the Mississippi and the Gulf of Mexico in the south. After the decision to retain Canada rather than one or more islands in the West Indies (a controversy, astonishing to the present generation), how was this new province, with its uncertain boundaries and with vast hinterlands stretching through the Great Lakes to the head-waters of the Ohio river and the Mississippi, and beyond through unknown spaces to the Pacific, to be incorporated into the British Empire? New France or Canada was inhabited by some eighty thousand French, alien from the thirteen Plantations to the south in race, religion, law, language, system of land tenure and outlook on life. The British in the St. Lawrence basin were a mere handful of foreign conquerors with a deeply rooted tradition of what today is called "self-determination." Was this handful to impose and maintain its principles by force on an overwhelming and antagonised majority, or was the negligible minority to accept a foreign system, so antagonistic to everything prevailing on the Atlantic seaboard and in the Motherland? It was a wholly new problem for which there were no precedents to guide either rulers or ruled.

Pass down by Albany and the Hudson river and you come to a huge area held by some two million men and women, eighty-five per cent of whom at least were British by race and almost all of whom were English in tongue. The annexation of Canada freed these two millions from the French menace and to that extent weakened the dependence on the

Home Government, but it accentuated the pressure of policy and administration, obvious before the war. Under Pitt there had been a surprising unity of effort to defeat France, but the winning of the war did not automatically win the peace, and history was now repeating itself. Unity of effort in war never has created, and never will create, a similar unity of effort in peace. The human mind requires a new objective and new springs of action, appropriate to the new conditions which victory has imposed. And these can only be given from above, by a government or a group of master minds correctly diagnosing the situation and ready to think out new lines of action.

Two questions were immediately urgent. How was the war to be paid for? How were the British Plantations to be defended? It was not unreasonable to expect a contribution from the colonists, the beneficiaries of victory, to the cost of the war, or to hold that defence was essentially an imperial duty and that if Great Britain provided the forces the colonists would find their pay and keep. And how urgent "defence" was Pontiac's Rebellion (of 1763), which took two years to extinguish, proved up to the hilt. But behind these two immediate needs lurked two clearly larger and more formidable issues.

The thirteen colonies were blocked to the west by the long range of the Alleghenies and Appalachian mountains reaching as far as the frontiers of Florida, now to be British, and the northern and most thickly populated seven had as their hinterland and "living space" precisely the territory which apparently was considered as part of western New France or Canada—the vast area from the Great Lakes to the Mississippi. But as population increased and land-hunger grew with it the colonists were penetrating the mountain barriers, filtering through into what seemed to be lands of milk and honey, inhabited only by ferocious Indians and countless buffaloes. With a people in whom the sap was steadily rising, it might be possible to direct or organise this inevitable expansion, but it was quite impossible to stop it. The pioneers, the backwoodsmen, the fur-traders, the *cour-*

eurs de bois, the landless with axe and musket would hack their way to the watersheds and then through the barriers of mountain, forest or river, for there was fat land to be had for the asking, and the blue horizon stretched illimitably westwards until, though they did not know it, the Mississippi provided Nature's boundary—for a time. These illiterate but tough men and women were turning their backs not only on Europe, but on their own folk and their traditions along the Atlantic sea-coast; what they were about to make was not new English Plantations but an America of English speech and a new mentality controlling the vast quadrilateral from New Orleans to the west end of Lake Superior at Duluth and covering today the States of Kentucky and West Virginia, Wisconsin, Michigan, Illinois, Indiana and Ohio, Tennessee and Alabama.

In 1763 the Home Government began to be seriously concerned. Somehow or other the movement westwards must be directed and controlled; the Indians had their rights, and a growing trade, which ought to be flowing from west to east but most perversely was flowing from north to south, must be brought into the mercantile framework of the British Empire, for trade meant revenue, and the need for more revenue was urgent.

The whole imperial system was in fact the major element of the problem. This had three aspects: first, the administrative relations between the Home Government and the several colonies; secondly, the economic aspect of "the mercantile system" on which the Empire was based; and thirdly, the imperial executive concerned with customs, the enforcement of the Trading and Navigation Acts and defence; but all three aspects blended with each other and made a single whole.

One conclusion is quite clear. The Stamp Act and Grenville's other administrative measures were not a wanton and unprovoked assault upon a system which until 1763 had worked effectively and harmoniously. Ever since 1714 there had been continuous friction, with the Home Government constantly (though for the most part impotently) intervening, to the resentment of the local legislatures, particularly as to whether the Governor, the Judges and such executive staff as there was should be independent of the local taxpayer for salary and office. The Trade Acts implied that trade was reserved to the British Empire and British shipping, that the colonies provided raw material, receiving manufactured goods in return, and that manufactures and trading with foreigners were either regulated by a high tariff or prohibited altogether. But as a matter of fact the mercantile system was either evaded, ignored or violated when it suited the individual colonist; "smuggling" was freely practised by the most respectable persons, and even trading with the enemy in time of war was not condemned, particularly if successful and profitable. And the lamentable truth stands out that the colonies grew up with no real respect for law and legal order which not only stained the record in the next twenty years but was the worst legacy of the successful revolution to the new United States in 1783.

The imperial administration (customs, smuggling, and so forth) fell mainly to the British Navy, but the weakness (or positive absence) of an executive for carrying out the system is conspicuous until the final rupture; nor was there in London a single department under a responsible minister of high status charged with "colonial" affairs. Distance, with the inevitable ignorance on both sides, was the root of the difficulties, for a despatch might take six months or more to come and return, even if answered at once, which seldom happened. Ministers and members of Parliament could not visit Massachusetts or Virginia (they did not visit Ireland, only 60, not 3,000, miles away) nor could Boston or Philadelphia visit Westminster. And on both sides misunderstandings were created which a day's conference between the leading parties could have dissolved. But the facile assumption that a rupture was inevitable and that colonies must, like ripe fruit, fall from the parent tree has no justification either in theory or in fact. "Inevitable results in history," truly says Prof. McIlwain, "are about the last resort of the despairing historian."

India simultaneously provided another wholly different

and complicated problem, for which, also, there was no precedent either in our history or that of any other country. Munro's victory at Buxar in 1764, in which the Mogul Empire and not merely a provincial Nawab was really defeated, much more than Plassey laid the foundation of British power. But, as Horace Walpole shrewdly remarked, "it was easier to conquer the East than to know what to do with it." We had gone to India in the reign of James I to trade, and through an increasingly powerful and chartered company built up a great commercial business, the agents of which were managers of trade and not administrators, colonists or settlers. They went out and came back as Pitt's grandfather had done to form the "Nabob" class at home, if they did not die, as many did, at their stations. Their formidable rivals were a French trading company, also there for commerce and not colonisation, and to a less degree the Dutch.

A new phase opened when French genius had brought in as allies the Indian Princes and Nawabs to oust the British and secure a monopoly for France, while the Mogul Empire with its capital at Delhi had gone slowly into dissolution. And now the British East India Company had not only vanquished both French and Dutch—though, be it noted, only with the help of an imperial navy and imperial troops —but had acquired military authority and criminal justice (Nizamat), together with taxing authority and civil justice (Diwani) over large areas hitherto under native rule. A great trading corporation had become a government.

How and on what principles was the East India Company to discharge its new administrative functions? Sovereignty under the British flag required the authority and orders of the Crown, through a minister responsible to Parliament. No one knew better than Pitt what the chartered powers of the directors and the East India House were, for had not his grandfather played a notorious part in defying or obeying both? When, therefore, in 1759, Clive wrote to Mr. Secretary Pitt a famous letter summing up the new situation and boldly proposing that the Crown should resume and exercise its rights in governing these new and large territories, the

Secretary of State, absorbed in the war, postponed all action, for it was, indeed, as he saw, "a nice question." But now in 1764-5 it must be dealt with. Deep and widespread vested interests were involved; charters renewable at stated intervals could be revised but could not be cancelled simply by an order in Council; who was to govern, and with what responsibility to whom? And was the Crown to obtain an increasing revenue, not granted or appropriated by the British legislature, but which would make the sovereign less dependent on the House of Commons, and enormously increase its resources in patronage and "corruption"? Knotty problems indeed in the days of Stamp Acts, "No taxation without representation," general warrants and *North Briton* attacks on Prerogative, and a Middlesex election and Wilkes just ahead.

There was, also, foreign policy. It was taken for granted by all who had eyes in their head that a humiliated France would (in co-operation with Spain) work for a war of "revenge," and that under Choiseul the menace of Bourbon power was as great as ever. The Treaty of Peace had scarcely scotched France, and its authors had alienated and thrown away the one ally round whom we could build a counter-system to the alliance of Versailles and Vienna. Pitt, who had denounced the treatment of Frederick, clung to his conviction that it was a fundamental British interest to link up London with Berlin and St. Petersburg, where a new, vigorous and "illuminated" empress, Catherine, over the corpse of a murdered and half-sane husband, was about to make herself "The Semiramis of the North." But it was not only Bute's clumsy bungling which had queered the pitch. Sacred egoism at Sans Souci might and did stridently pose as the victim of British treachery. In reality Frederick was convinced that Great Britain was no longer of any use to him. The interest of Prussia lay on its eastern frontiers; loot and living space could reconcile Vienna, St. Petersburg and Berlin, and three monarchies could consolidate a new friendship by sharing the chaotic Naboth's Vineyard on the borders of all three— Poland, and for this purpose Great Britain was not merely of no value, but might be an uncomfortable obstacle. Pitt—yes, a great man, no doubt, but who could guarantee either his health or his tenure of office, after his treatment in 1761? And there was the rub.

Two events had happened which, like the ships in the Persian war with Greece, were the origin and cause of all the subsequent troubles. On April 30th, 1763, a Secretary of State, Lord Halifax, had issued a general warrant against John Wilkes, a member of Parliament, and others concerned for a "false, malicious and scandalous libel" in No. 45 of *The North Briton*: on March 22nd, 1765, the Royal Assent was given to "the Stamp Act" (5 Geo. III, c. 12) "for granting and applying certain stamp duties, and other duties, in the British Colonies and plantations in America towards further defraying the expenses of defending, protecting and securing the same." The first raised fundamental principles of constitutional law, together with the nature of Parliamentary privilege; the second, as the preamble quoted above shows, asserted the right of the Crown in Parliament at Westminster to tax the American colonies without first obtaining their assent. London since 1763, the Colonies since 1765, were now in an uproar.

3. William Pitt: 1765–1770

On both the issues Pitt made his views unmistakably clear. Detesting, as he did, Wilkes' violence of language and libertine morals, he opposed the Resolutions in the House of Commons which declared that Privilege of Parliament did not extend to "seditious libel," and that "the said John Wilkes be expelled," and he deplored the action of the House of Lords in concurring in these Resolutions, as an unwarrantable intervention by the Upper into the affairs and rights of the Lower House and wholly agreed with the vigorous Protest of seventeen peers recorded in the Lords Journals for November 29th, 1763; while he rejoiced in the judicial decisions, notably that by Lord Camden in *Entick* v. *Carrington*, which finally decided the illegality of general warrants, and dismissed the "argument of state necessity" with the observation that "the Common Law does not understand that kind of reasoning," Pitt, in fact, led the opposition with such vehemence and success that on February 17th, 1764, the majority for the Government was down to fourteen. The gladiator of 1755 had reappeared in 1763 challenging the attack of the administration on fundamental principles of liberty; and then in March 1764 gout and depression struck him down and he did not return to Parliament for nearly two years (January 1766), so that he was not "in his place" when the Stamp Act was passed in a languid House. It was more than unfortunate, for he might have prevented that unhappy measure from ever reaching the Statute Book.

When he did return, the Rockingham ministry was in office, and again he made his attitude crystal clear in the first of his big speeches on the American colonies. For Pitt the imperial system involved two principles: the right of the imperial Parliament to regulate trade, prohibit manufactures, if necessary, and tax by customs, tariff or any other imposition and take the revenue accruing therefrom for such purposes as the legislature thought fit; the inherent and inalienable right of the colonial legislatures was to impose internal taxation. The Stamp Act imposed internal taxation and, therefore, was not merely impolitic but constitutionally a breach of the right of the taxpayer alike in North America as in Great Britain. And he asserted in a single sentence what for him was a fundamental base of his position—from that day in 1766 until his death twelve years later: "if liberty be not countenanced in America it will sicken, fade and die in this country." In a sentence which was never to be forgotten on either side of the Atlantic, Pitt "rejoiced that America has resisted," and when the Stamp Act was repealed, and, on his motion, all general warrants (April 25th) were declared illegal, he could write to his devoted Hester almost lyrically. But it was more than regrettable, as subsequent events showed, that he did not prevent the passing of the Declaratory Act (6 Geo. III, c. 12), which with explicit emphasis proclaimed that the Crown in Parliament, "had, hath and ought to have full power and authority to make laws to bind the colonies, in all cases whatsoever." Pitt, probably, thought that after the experience of 1765 and 1766 the blunder of the Stamp Act would never be repeated. He did not foresee that, when the blunder was repeated, he would either not be at Westminster or impotent to prevent it.

The Rockingham ministry was too weak to last. Appealed to by the King, Pitt consented (July 17th) to form, on his own principles, a national government in which Temple, for the second time, refused to have any part. The result was the Cabinet based on "destroying all party distinctions," of Burke's famous description,[3] in which the Duke of Grafton, immortalised by "Junius," and even more "the slave" of Pitt than he was of Nancy Parsons, was First Lord of the Treasury; and Pitt, taking an earldom, was Lord Privy Seal, but recognised by everyone as the real Master of the Ministry. The tessellated mosaic was a deliberate act, offensive as it was to all the "groups" and "factions" because Pitt intended to be, with the King's unquestioned approval, as efficient a director of this, his last, administration as he had been of his first in 1757.

But when it became known that "the Great Commoner" was leaving the Lower, to take his place in the Upper, House there was a prolonged wail of dismay, which Gray, in his hermit's cell at Cambridge, sincerely voiced and which was the prelude to a snowfall of squibs and lampoons. The new Lord Privy Seal had probably two reasons for his peerage and office—health and pride. He felt that he must be relieved from the strain of an exacting administrative post together with the long hours and excitement of the House of Commons. His love of pomp, ceremony and circumstance was now gratified and an earldom put him on a level with his most arrogant brother-in-law, Temple, and with any other political or social rival. And quite recently (1765) the act of

---

[3] "Such a diversified piece of mosaic: such a tessellated pavement without cement; here a bit of black stone, and there a bit of white; patriots and courtiers, King's friends and republicans, Whigs and Tories, treacherous friends and open enemies."

an eccentric admirer had made him a landowner, by the bequest of the estate of Burton Pynsent, in Somerset, reputed to be worth at least £3,000 a year, with its mansion, park, farms and tenants, to which with his usual financial reckless-ness the new landlord at once set to develop on his own standard of what was fit for an earl and Lord Privy Seal. One more burden of management and debt was, thereby, added to the cares of Lady Chatham, striving in a multiplicity of tasks to keep the peace between her brothers and her husband.

Justify it as easily as we may, the peerage was a profound mistake. Pitt's power of inspiring, guiding and concentrating public opinion within and without the Palace of Westminster rested on his membership of the House of Commons. Speeches, however eloquent and unanswerable, in a chilly and hostile House of Lords could alter neither policy nor votes nor rally public opinion. When he ceased to be "the Great Commoner," Pitt was Samson with his locks cut—by himself.

In August 1766, Chatham (as he now must be to the end of the chapter) set to work with demonic energy to tackle the major problems demanding solution, above all France and India. "The entire overthrow of the French system" was one main objective, for Choiseul was skilfully reorganising the French navy, army and commerce for another and victorious war of revenge, and another was a drastic in-vestigation of the abuses in the administration of the East India Company, leading to a revision of the charter and the functions of the Corporation. In Cabinet Charles Townshend, the Chancellor of the Exchequer, the new darling of the House of Commons and of White's Club, noted how the Lord Privy Seal impressed his colleagues with his "transcendent superiority" and made them feel "what inferior animals they were." But everywhere it was, also, noted that these col-leagues were treated simply as subordinates to carry out a "sole Minister's" policy and that Chatham's arrogance, haughty bearing, irritability and resentment of any criticism or opposition increased daily, while his wife and relatives were embarrassed by personal extravagance in building, and the horde of retainers required for his domestic establishment.

A physical and mental breakdown was at hand, and it came in January 1767. It was called "gout" or a failure to develop gout and clear the system, but it really was an attack of manic-depressive insanity (which had, also, already shown itself in the King, in 1765) with its profound melancholia and deceptive lucid intervals, aggravated by gout and probably Bright's disease. The Lord Privy Seal ceased to function; he or Lady Chatham on his behalf refused to see Grafton (save once) or any of his colleagues or to answer piteous appeals for guidance; in October 1768, he insisted on resigning, against the emphatic wish of the King, and though in April 1769 he had recovered sufficiently to be reconciled to Temple, it was not until July of that year that, like a ghost from a forgotten past, he astonished the world of St. James's and Westminster by appearing at a royal levee.

These two years of collapse, the most serious in his gout-ridden life, were fatal to Chatham, to his ministry and to the British Empire. To many like Lord George Sackville he was (and truly enough) simply "mad"; to others who heard of his riding or driving at times he was, for inscrutable reasons, simply a malingerer; to Burke, the mouthpiece of "the Rockinghams," he was "on his back talking fustian," while devoted adherents such as Grafton and Shelburne praying for advice and leadership were like sheep who had lost their shepherd, and weak-kneed followers such as Lord Camden and Conway accepted in Cabinet what they knew was wrong but had not the courage either to oppose or to resign. But if Chatham recovered, one devoted woman, Hester Grenville, who had never despaired of her lord's power to be himself again, was the worker of the miracle. On July 6th, 1769, the King received Chatham in private audience, when the former Minister plainly expressed his disapproval of all that had happened or been done in his absence. George III listened and said nothing. It was Chatham's last audience and the two never met again.

4. Wilkes and the American Problem

When Chatham returned to the world of the living he found that not only in every sphere, foreign, colonial and domestic, grave issues had been raised but that the whole political scene had been altered. Stage and players were new, the atmosphere and mentality were quite different, and his last eight years were to be played out, as happens from time to time in a people's history, with mediocrity triumphant and a political world which refused to recognise realities that did not fit in with its own delusive diagnosis, until the collapse of the structure of its imagination brought it into collision with facts that could neither be denied nor ignored. "The President of the Immortals, in Aeschylean phrase," does not "sport" with his mortal playthings, nor does he drive them mad before he destroys them; but he seals their eyes and stops their ears, until their eyes, as his, are once again upon the Truth.

In 1769 Chatham was in his sixty-first year, and the men he had fought or worked with had mostly gone—Anson in 1762, Carteret (Granville) in 1763, Hardwicke and Legge in 1764, Cumberland in 1765, Charles Townshend in 1767, Newcastle in 1768, and in 1770 George Grenville, Ligonier, Beckford and Granby were to disappear. Of the first line Mansfield and Camden almost alone remained. Bute was nourishing his rancour in internment at his new palace of Luton Hoo, and Henry Fox, when not at Kingsgate hungering and intriguing for an earldom, was ruining his brilliant son, Charles James Fox, at the gaming table. The young King was in his thirty-first year, and of the Whigs, Rockingham and Richmond, and the ablest, Shelburne, mistrusted by everybody, were young enough to be Chatham's sons. For Chatham might have anticipated the just judgment of his second son, William, some thirty years later, when tackled about his colleagues. "What," he is reported to have replied, "are you to do with skim milk like that?" Chatham had come back to find a Treasury Bench of skim milk.

The tessellated ministry of 1766 split into its speckled pieces and dissolved: and the residuary legatee of its power and authority was George III. For the personal monarchy of "the Patriot King" dates not from 1760 but from 1769 after the corrupt General Election of 1768. George in nine years had learnt his job; if he did not attend meetings of the Cabinet he was the real prime and sole minister from whom the departmental chiefs took their orders; he had mastered as completely as Newcastle the machinery and technique of administration, of elections, places, pensions and the Secret Service List, and, unlike Newcastle, no cabal or "factious" combination could turn him out, while he was the fountain of everything that men or women might desire, peerages and ribbons, sinecures or doles, bishoprics, deaneries or Crown livings (to be held by absentees), grooms of the chamber, waiting women of Her Majesty's household, gold sticks or holders of the Copper Kettle—the King knew them all and distributed them strictly for value—a vote in either Chamber of Parliament or in a Crown, Admiralty or Pocket Borough; the voting lists in the divisions of the House of Commons were daily studied at Kew House and "defaulters" noted; resignation of your post without royal permission was sedition or desertion, neither forgotten nor forgiven; and there was no reversionary interest to offer a rival promissory note that might not be cashed; and the only possible Cave of Adullam was the cradles in the royal nursery which Her Gracious Majesty continued to fill with exemplary regularity.

In pure politics the King had three outstanding advantages: he was as industrious as a beaver building his dam; he was a model of the domestic virtues, for no woman, until he went definitely mad, ever obtained from him either a penny or the flicker of an eyelid; and when he had made up his mind, he was like the famous Tweeny, "nothink would budge him." In addition he had an uncanny shrewdness in estimating situations or a person, in driving a bargain and in handling the pieces on the chessboard. Of real statesmanship, of imagination or comprehension of great issues, as of gratitude, he knew nothing.

In 1769, by patience and never throwing away an opportunity, he had a ministry obedient to his will, with a docile majority in both Houses of Parliament, voting for or rejecting as they were instructed by the Royal instruments on the Government Bench, while in January 1770 he had found a First Lord of the Treasury after his heart, Lord North, an admirable debater, well fitted to be Prime Minister in Laodicea, and whom only one man, a groom, had ever been known to make angry. And outside administration was a handful of great territorials, clinging to such Whig principles as were daily called from the minarets of Grosvenor Square by the Grand Mufti, Edmund Burke, and behind them another handful of city rebels who to those born in the purple of Mayfair were almost untouchables. Both groups pined for a leader—and now the Lost Leader had come back, or had he not?

Chatham found a record eloquent of dissension within and blunders without. The army had dropped back to its weakness in 1756, the fleet was not being kept up and the Royal Dockyards were allowed to become sinks of inefficiency, political graft and financial corruption. Choiseul, now that Pitt was no longer there to terrify either Versailles or Madrid, had in 1768 annexed Corsica, just in time for a baby christened Napoleon Bonaparte in 1769 to be registered as a French citizen, and had thereby established a new naval base over against the lost Minorca. But the real evil genius had been "the new luminary" Charles Townshend, Chancellor of the Exchequer, brilliant, fascinating and irresistibly reckless, dealing with the two big problems of imperial policy—India and the American colonies.

Instead of the drastic investigation of the East India Company's rights and functions leading up to a fundamental settlement of the relations of the Crown as the authority for government and the Company as a trading corporation, Townshend dealt directly with the directors on the basis of "their right to all territorial revenue," and shored up the trading organisation in its grave financial embarrassment, so that an opportunity of solving great imperial issues on principles and not on patchwork expediency and dubious vested rights was thrown way. Even more serious, Townshend made good his pledge to tax the colonies by an external imposition (and free, therefore, from the defects of Grenville's proposals), undo the effect of the repeal of the Stamp Act, assert the right laid down in the Declaratory Act and restore and enforce the supreme authority of the Crown in Parliament to legislate for North America. On July 2nd, 1767, the royal assent was given to measures which laid duties on tea, glass, paper, red and white lead paints and so forth to be levied in the ports at the colonies, and provide for a Civil List, independent of the local assemblies; at Boston an American Customs Board was to be set up for restricting smuggling, and the New York Assembly was suspended until that colony complied with the recently imposed Mutiny Act. The total amount of the new revenue was to be no more than £40,000—but Townshend's proposals challenged every principle of the colonial opposition. Having thus wrought the maximum of mischief in a minimum of time, the Chancellor of the Exchequer, whose "champagne speech" on May 8th had intoxicated all "the King's Friends," took to his bed and died on September 4th of "a neglected fever." If only it had been the colonies and not a fever that he had "neglected"!

More immediate in its effects was "the Middlesex Election." Wilkes had returned from abroad in February 1768, stood for the City of London to be defeated and was then elected for Middlesex, but was expelled by the Commons on February 17th, 1769. Twice he was re-elected unopposed; standing again he polled 1043 to 296 votes for his opponent Colonel Luttrell. By a famous resolution the House of Commons (April 15th) declared that Luttrell "ought to have been returned" and inserted his name in the return as "duly elected"; London and Middlesex were at once in an uproar with "Wilkes and Liberty," as their war-cry. And the controversy passed permanently into our literature when "Junius" (whose identity has never been established beyond question) issued the *Letters,* in their venomous polish taking their place beside Swift's more subtle but not less polished sarcasm.

Wilkes was instrumental in raising (in 1771) another subject of fierce controversy—the publication of debates in Parliament—when, as an alderman of the City of London, with the Lord Mayor, Brass Crosby, he defied the House of Commons' attempt to regard publication as a breach of privilege. Though on the technical legal point the Court of Common Pleas decided against Wilkes and Crosby, the House tacitly admitted defeat in the storm its action had roused, and after 1771 ceased to enforce the privilege it had claimed.

Chatham for two years after his return was in the forefront of the violent battles that rent London and public opinion and was able to lead a united opposition on the Middlesex election; his signature is one of the forty-two to a weighty Protest in the Journals of the House of Lords (February 2nd, 1770), exposing the menace to liberty of the "suspending and dispensing power assumed and exercised by the House of Commons"; he proclaimed his intention of being a "scarecrow of violence to the gentle warblers of the grove"; he demanded (but in vain) a dissolution which would sweep away the tyrannical majority in the Lower House and end the "corrupting" power of "royal influence," and, most notable of all, he made Parliamentary "reform" a central point in "remedial measures."

While the boroughs, the evil part of the electoral system, must be left alone, the pure and free element, viz. the counties, should be strengthened by the addition of a third member to each county, and in addition Chatham declared himself "a convert to Triennial Parliaments," and for the repeal of the Septennial Act. It suffices here to note that from the date of these utterances Parliamentary Reform anticipated the creed of the new Whiggism, born in 1771, though it was not till two years after Chatham's death that, in 1780, it was rebaptised and adopted as an article of a revised Whig faith.

On two other issues, also, Chatham emphatically challenged North's ministry. In 1769 and 1770, Mansfield (in the cases of *Almon* and *Woodfall*) had laid it down that in trials for criminal libel the function of the jury was simply to decide the fact of "publication," and that of the judge to decide whether the matter was libellous. Supported by Camden, Chatham fiercely attacked Mansfield's interpretation of the law, for he foresaw, as a judge declared a century later, that "the jury," limited in their powers, could not be "the true guardians of the liberty of the Press," and he read in Mansfield's decision only another example of the Government's assault on freedom of speech as one of "the ancient and fundamental liberties of the Kingdom." The challenge failed, and it was not until 1792 that Fox's Libel Act settled the dispute as Chatham so passionately desired twenty years earlier.

The continuous danger from the Bourbon monarchies was the prime article of Chatham's foreign policy. When, therefore, Spain in 1770 ejected the British (sent out by himself in 1766) from Port Egmont in the Falkland Islands he demanded insistently that the action should be disavowed and the British occupation recognised, and that it should be made clear to Versailles that intervention by France in an Anglo-Spanish dispute would not be tolerated. The danger of war was averted by the dismissal of Choiseul (thanks probably to the new *maîtresse-en-titre*, Du Barry) and the British flag was restored.

The importance of this episode lies in three points: Chatham's correct diagnosis that Versailles and Madrid would seize any and every favourable opportunity to reverse the defeat of 1763; his repeated emphasis on "the clear self-evident impossibility for this country to contend with the united power of the House of Bourbon, merely upon the strength of its own resources"; and the growing danger due to the reorganisation of their military strength by the Bourbon powers and a steady decline, especially in the efficiency and numbers of the British Fleet. For the plain truth was that since 1763 Great Britain had really retired from the Continent, was without an ally in Europe, while her navy was no longer on a two-power, and scarcely on a single-power, standard. Twelve months later the victorious Great Britain of 1763, ignored, impotent and indifferent, had to witness the successful First Partition of Poland (1772), and four years later the intervention of France and the loss of the command of the seas in the civil war in North America.

Vigorous and invigorating as his political campaign had been on all points, Chatham recognised his failure and retired from London, disillusioned and embittered. It had really been a duel between him and the King, and the King had won, for it was the King's control and leadership that alone had kept the serried ministerial majority in both Houses of Parliament intact and even confident. The Whigs had lost their ablest member in George Grenville and Chatham his chief liaison officer with "the City" in Beckford; the rioting and violence of "demagogic language" in London and Middlesex terrified the great territorial magnates such as Rockingham, and to the aristocracy of Mayfair Wilkes was a repulsive ally, nor had they any stomach for Parliamentary "reform." The heat and flame of 1769–1771 cooled rapidly, and for the next three years, while England sank into an ignoble apathy,[4] Chatham was absent, wrestling with the results of his own extravagance at Burton Pynsent, and his incurable habit of extinguishing debt by fresh and bigger debt, with repeated bouts of serious illness, and with the education of his children, particularly his second son, William, born in the Year of Victory, 1759, "the hope and comfort of my life," who was not allowed to go either to Eton or Westminster, but who at fourteen was sent up to Pembroke College, Cambridge.

But neither Chatham nor anyone else grasped what was probably the most serious result of the years from 1769 to 1774, the effect on the mind of the colonist in North America. What men think, reasonably or unreasonably, is more decisive than what they ought to, but do not, think. Month by

[4] "A gaming, robbing, wrangling, railing nation, without principles, genius, character or allies; the overgrown shadow of what it was." (Horace Walpole.)

month as the news reached New York, Philadelphia, Boston or Richmond the conviction grew that "coercion" in the colonies was the complement to a royal and ministerial plan to destroy liberty and the rights to a free and self-governing people in the Motherland; and that a corrupted Parliament in London could only mean corrupted assemblies in the colonies. In all major controversies the most fatal feature is distrust in the parties concerned of each other's honesty and sincerity. And distrust was now growing like a poisonous weed on both sides of the Atlantic.

5. The Imperial and Colonial Problem: 1770–1776

"One single Act of Parliament (the Stamp Act) has set people a-thinking more than they had done in all their lives"— (Otis in 1765); "When a great question is first started, there are very few, even of the greatest minds, which suddenly and intuitively comprehend it, in all its consequences"—(Novanglus, (J. Adams), January 1775); "The Management of so complicated and mighty a machine as the United Colonies requires the meekness of Moses, the patience of Job and the wisdom of Solomon, added to the valour of David"—(John Adams, April 1776).

These three quotations illuminate the forces working under the surface of the colonial mind during ten momentous years.

For two years and a half, after the winter of 1770–1, Chatham took no decisive part in public affairs. He only made one speech (May 1772), and that was in favour of releasing Dissenters from subscription (under the Toleration Act of 1689) to certain of the Thirty-Nine Articles—a speech notable for its emphasis on a fundamental of his political faith. "I am," he declared, "for this bill" (which had been passed in the Commons), "because I am for toleration, that sacred right of nature and bulwark of truth." But the Bench of Bishops in the Upper House was too strong and the proposal was rejected by 102 to 29 votes.

India absorbed much of his interest. Fiercely indignant with the notorious abuses in the administration of the East India

Company, "so rank as to stink to earth and heaven," he supported North's Regulation Act of 1773, which imposed a modest control both on the governmental and financial autonomy of the Company, against the views of Burke and the Whigs, to whom "chartered rights" were sacrosanct. It was certainly not the solution for which he had hoped in the happier days of 1766, for North's bill really evaded the basic issue—the resumption of the rights of the Crown and the responsibility for government to the Crown in Parliament and not to a Board of Directors. And here again we find the major chord of all Chatham's statesmanship struck with no uncertain hand: "The hearts and good affections of Bengal are of more worth than all the profits of ruinous and odious monopolies" —language both unintelligible and dangerous to East India House and Change Alley. Imperial policy, in other words, is not an affair merely of law, prescription or precedent. It must deal with the heart and mind, and from the memory pluck a rooted sorrow.

These two central principles—the *idées maîtresses*—are the core, though not the sum, of his policy on the colonial and imperial problem in North America, to which from April 1774 to his death in May 1778 he devoted his ebbing physical strength and shattered body. And these four years of failure are as great in their own way as the four years of triumphant war from 1757 to 1761. The Chatham of 1774 was already a broken man, in everything but spirit and insight. Could he have been the Pitt of 1756 and in the House of Commons, the final result would assuredly have not been what it was.

A deceptive calm, save in Massachusetts, prevailed, and at home it was generally thought that the troubles with the colonies were over. Crown and ministerialists were rudely and quickly undeceived. North's government had repealed all the Townshend duties, retaining only a three-penny tax on tea, on which the East India Company was to get a drawback; on December 16th, 1773, a small band led by Sam Adams attacked the East India liners at Boston and destroyed the imported tea, while a large crowd looked on in silent sympathy ("the Boston Tea Party"). This to the Home Government was not merely riot and defiance of law, of which there had been much since 1763, but "rebellion," and severe "coercive" measures were promptly passed—the Port of Boston was closed; the charter of Massachusetts was suspended and drastically revised; four regiments were sent to the Commander, Gage, to support his authority; compulsory billeting was imposed on Boston, and offenders against "order" were to be removed for trial to Nova Scotia. The reaction in the other colonies was immediate and ominous; and after a notable meeting in the Raleigh Tavern in Virginia the First Continental Congress, at which every colony, save Georgia, was represented, was held (September 5th) at Philadelphia. Support to Massachusetts in resistance to "the Coercive Acts" was unanimously adopted, and a boycotting non-importation of British goods on the lines of a similar movement in 1765 was readily agreed to. The date and the place are important. At Philadelphia in 1774 a Revolutionary Legislature had been born.

Fear, distrust and opposition in the colonies had been strengthened by the Quebec Act passed at Westminster in this memorable year, 1774. This measure, on the true assumption that for a long time to come "Canada" must remain French in language, religion and social institutions and that it was unwise, if not impossible, to give it the self-government obtaining in the English colonies of North America, recognised the French civil law as authoritative, legalised the payment of tithes to the Roman Catholic Church and brought a huge hinterland south and west of the Great Lakes within the boundaries of the Province, which was to be administered by a Governor, appointed by, and a council largely nominated by, the Crown. In fact, the Act was a statutory recognition of an alien nationalism within the Empire, and, surprising in 1774, was an effort to reconcile "the foreign body" to the imperial system of Great Britain. But to the colonies it was anathema, without qualification, one more signal proof of the deep "ministerial plan for enslaving us." The recognition of the Roman Catholic Church was hateful; administration as prescribed was an extension of the "tyrannical" system, made clear by the suspension of the Massachusetts Charter, while the defined limits of this area of "absolute government" robbed the seven northern colonies of the territory, implicitly granted them in their charters, into which they would naturally expand.

Chatham, to whom every concession to anything French was dangerous and was almost the strongest element in his political creed, voiced in London the opposition of the colonists. It was difficult for him to think out a policy for an entirely new situation, which his conduct of the war had created, and with his experience of the controversies at home he shared the deep suspicions of the colonists of the ulterior objectives of the bill. From North's ministry no good measure could be expected. For all his imaginative insight Chatham did not see that the whole imperial issue from the basin of the St. Lawrence to the boundaries of Florida had been so altered that a wholly different framework and principles of government were urgently needed.

The Quebec Act passed. It did not inaugurate a new system, for it was only an effort to provide a workable administration for a large area in which the British were a tiny handful, but it bridged over a difficult dilemma. By the recognition of the landowning seigneurs and of French civil law and of the powerful Roman Catholic Church it reconciled the French population to British rule and the sovereignty of the British Crown. Only two years later the French, whom we had fought from 1757 to 1763, were repelling an invasion from the revolted American colonists and defeating the plan to "free" and cut Canada out of the Empire and unite it with the English "America" to the south. North's ministry cannot be credited with a stroke of prescient statesmanship, otherwise a "Quebec Act" for Ireland might have successfully solved that important problem in imperial policy, which was also becoming urgent. In history mediocrity endeavouring simply to paper over obvious and large cracks in the walls at times stumbles unawares into a success it has neither anticipated nor deserved. North's ministry listened to Carleton, the man on the spot at Quebec. If only they had, after 1774, continued to listen to him and to others as wise farther south! With the end of the year 1774 the controversy in North America had reached a climax, and looking back now we can see the phases through which it had passed and the nature of the crisis requiring the gravest and most momentous decisions.

As has been pointed out, the Peace Treaty of 1763 had imposed, apart from the imperial system of government, an urgent practical problem: how was the war to be paid for? how was defence to be provided? Neither as individual units nor collectively were the colonists ready to contribute, and they had a seventeenth-century fear and dislike of a "standing army" outside colonial authority and under a special code of law, which could be used to enforce an irresponsible executive authority. The resistance to the Stamp Act came as a great surprise to the Home Government and even to many in the colonies. "No taxation without representation" became the watchword. But the repeal of the Stamp Act and the passing of the Declaratory Act (1766) were doubly unfortunate. They taught the colonists that resistance had only to be obstinate enough to be successful, and they had provoked a statement of the legislative power of the Crown in Parliament so explicit as to transform any future resistance into a repudiation of the principle, so defined.

It is generally agreed that in 1765 there was no party already working for separation, but unquestionably a minority led by Sam Adams and Patrick Henry was determined to pare down to such a minimum all imperial control as to make the colonies virtually independent; and, as all revolutions exemplify, a minority knowing exactly what it wants and how it can be got will, particularly if strengthened by continuous provocation, dominate even a large majority, ignorant, puzzled and uncertain of its own position in a controversy. Invariably, a point is then reached at which the minority well in advance of public opinion finds itself suddenly passed by a tidal wave of emotion and obliged to adopt a programme considerably beyond what it originally demanded. In eleven years this point was reached in the surge of sentiment that culminated in the Declaration of Independence of July 4th, 1776.

After 1766 there was much thinking and writing, and the controversy over the distinction between internal and external taxation had deepened into consideration of fundamental constitutional principles and an examination of the title deeds of the "liberties" and "rights" of the colonists as English subjects of the Crown. Before long on both sides of the Atlantic it became clear that two opposed and irreconcilable theories and interpretations of the whole imperial system were in issue.

The "unitarians" (as they may be called), exemplified at their best by a great lawyer such as Mansfield, held that the Empire was a unity, in which the Crown in Parliament had the same supreme authority outside the Realm (i.e. in the Dominions overseas) as in the Realm itself of Great Britain and Ireland; that this had been made clear both in 1649 and in 1689, and was the principle correctly laid down in the Declaratory Act of 1766, and was the principle on which the Crown at Westminster could and did legislate over the head, if necessary, of the Parliament in Dublin. It was, also, the principle on which the whole economic system (external taxation) of "mercantilism" was based. Denial of it was "rebellion," a repudiation of the sovereignty of the Crown, which, unless rooted out, must lead to the political and administrative disintegration of the whole imperial structure.

Against this theory the colonists developed a powerful argument (as Molyneux had done in the case of Ireland) that there was a clear distinction between the Crown "within the Realm" and the Crown "without the Realm" in the "Dominions thereunto belonging," and that the authority of the latter was only binding so far as any "Dominion" had accepted the acts of the Crown in Parliament within the Realm. Where there was no such acceptance the authority was invalid. The Charters, for example, were lawful acts of the Crown by its Prerogative outside the Realm accepted and operative as such. The colonists in North America had, as all English subjects, fundamental and inalienable rights of which, without their expressed assent, they could not be deprived by the Crown "within the Realm" operating in the Parliament at Westminster. The Stamp Act and any similar measure were legislation by a body in which they were not represented and were denials of a fundamental right to regulate the internal policy inherent in each member of every colony. It followed on this interpretation of the British Constitution that the real grievance of the Americans was not against the Sovereign as such, allegiance and obedience to whom were due and readily admitted, but against the Crown in Parliament, misled by evil ministers, making claims contrary to the character of the whole Constitution.

The economic system of imperial trade was certainly not the cause of the "revolt," nor was its abolition a prime article of the colonial case; for at the height of the controversy it seems to have been agreed, even by the minority extremists, that some general control of imperial trade as a whole was essential and beneficial and that an implicit consent to that control might be assumed without impairing the opposition to the authority of the Crown in Parliament at Westminster over "the Dominions without the Realm."

Chatham's attitude from 1765 onwards was perfectly clear and never altered. He accepted without qualification the right of the Imperial Parliament to regulate trade and, if necessary, forbid any colony to manufacture so much as a door-nail or a horse-shoe; he denied without qualification the right to impose internal taxation, which could only be granted by the competent representative assembly, and he "rejoiced" in the resistance to any such claim; he saw in ministerial measures in America the same spirit and objectives as he saw in the struggle at home over general warrants, freedom of speech and the Middlesex election: a ministerial victory in one sphere would mean a similar victory in the other. But, apart from the battle over "rights" in the defined cases of collision, Chatham emphasised his profound conviction that the controversy was not a question of law and of "the statute book turned down in dog's-ears," but of policy and statesmanship. We were in controversy with men and women of our own blood, speech and constitutional rights, who felt, thought and acted as we in the Motherland did or ought to, and we must deal with their minds and feelings and not merely with their rights or ours. A sincere spirit in Whitehall of "affection" would be met with a sincere spirit in Boston, New York and Philadelphia. And it is demonstrable that down to 1774 statements in protest and petitions enumerating explicit grievances were wholly directed against the Crown in Parliament, advised by ministers assuming authority for Acts of Parliament which in the nature of the Constitution it had not got. In a word, the colonists were really claiming what to-day we call "Dominion Status."

Between these two interpretations, if pursued, as they came to be, to their logical conclusions, neither compromise nor reconciliation was possible. The controversy passed from discussion of law and "natural rights" into the sphere of policy and of force. One of the parties must accept the interpretation of the other, which could in the case of refusal only be imposed and maintained by force—by Great Britain through the navy, army and imperial executive, by the colonists through a successful rebellion, ending in separation and the establishment of a new state, independent in principle and fact of the British Crown.

The successive subjects of controversy between 1765 and 1772 necessarily fell into a subsidiary position. The distinction between internal and external taxation, the claim or its repudiation that the colonies were virtually or indirectly represented in the legislature at Westminster, the terms of tenure of governors or judges in each colony, the financial needs of defence—all these "grievances" or demands—increased or kept alive the irritation and inflammation on both sides of the Atlantic; but once the fundamental and major issue had been raised the explicit claim in the Declaration Act of 1766 remained for acceptance or rejection. Were the colonists subject to the supreme authority of the Crown in Parliament at Westminster or were they only subject to the prerogative of the Crown (whatever that might be) in the Dominions without the Realm and for such legislation or taxation as the local legislature accepted?

Chatham was distressed, as were most of the opposition, by the lawless rioting, mob-violence and widespread persecution of "Tories" by "Whigs," particularly in the northern colonies, which strengthened the ministerial majority and hardened public opinion at home; but he was convinced that this deplorable conduct would disappear once you had removed the legitimate grievance which caused it.

And, with Chatham, there was behind the controversy, grave as that was, a gnawing and increasing fear, which he openly expressed, that unless America was appeased the Bourbon powers of France and Spain would seize the heaven-sent opportunity to reopen a war of revenge and Great Britain would once again have to fight a war for existence, but this time with a revolted America on her most vulnerable flank. And Chatham was right. Since July 1774 the place of Choiseul had been taken by Vergennes, the ablest foreign minister from the days of Torcy to the Revolution epoch, who shared Choiseul's views and was watching the situation with the keenest of eyes and wide knowledge of European affairs. Pressed by the young aristocrat liberals such as La Fayette and Rochambeau to aid "the rebels," Vergennes paused. Internally France was in a very bad state: support to "rebels" by an absolutist monarchy, already suffering from corrosive criticism, was dangerous; and if Great Britain crushed colonial "rebellion," France would have to face that Great Britain probably with Chatham, a name of terror, once again in power. "The Vulture of Versailles," as Chatham called her, must wait before pouncing and be sure that it was a dying beast in which it could fix its beak and talons.

It is clear that Chatham never fully grasped the realities and complexity of the imperial problem; his distinction between internal and external taxation was both logically and legally untenable and almost impossible to maintain in practice, for the "Boston Tea Party" was an attack on external taxation the validity of which, as an essential part of the imperial fabric, was a fundamental of his position: nor did he realise the perplexing truth that by 1765 the imperial system was out of date and that two millions of Americans, a nation in fact both of consumers and producers, could no longer be governed and retained within a weak and worn-out administrative framework and contested first principles of law and sovereignty.

It is safe to conclude that had Chatham since 1766 been in power he would either have withdrawn every measure offensive to the Americans or never proceeded to "coercive acts," and with the prestige and authority of his name and achievements persuaded the Americans to return to the system prior to 1765. But in 1775 no such policy would have removed the fundamental issue between the principle of the Declaratory Act and the constitutional claim to "Dominion Status." Once that was raised, civil war or a complete reconstruction of the imperial system was the only solution. Chatham, who saw no need for such a reconstruction and continued to think to the end in the categories of an eighteenth-century Whig statesman, would almost certainly have postponed the day of separation and ensured that at least it would not have come after a bitter civil war and by the drastic surgery of 1783 which poisoned for more than a century the relations of the English-speaking people on both sides of the Atlantic. But not even Chatham could have maintained the old order permanently.

It was on these lines that he worked from 1773 onwards against the ministerialists who were stronger in 1774, both in sentiment and numbers, than in 1766. He sought counsel and instruction from those who had first-hand knowledge, and particularly Franklin, the most versatile and intellectually gifted American of the eighteenth century. And Franklin had good reason to resent ministerial policy, for early in 1774 he had been publicly branded at the Privy Council by the brutal Wedderburn as a thief and a traitor.[5] He returned to his

---

[5] Franklin had obtained a bundle of letters written by Governor Hutchinson and showing that the Governor had advised most of the measures resented by the colonists, and allowed them to become known. He always maintained that his object in so doing was to prove that the origin of the "Coercion" was American and not English. The Assembly of Massachusetts petitioned for Hutchinson's removal, and when the matter came before the Privy Council, the Attorney-General, Wedderburn, denounced

lodging, folded up the brown suit he had worn and vowed he would only wear it again when he signed a document meeting the American demands in full.

Chatham embodied his proposals in a bill submitted to the House of Lords on February 1, 1775: he made his preamble an explicit assertion of the right of Parliament in all matters touching the general weal of the whole Dominion of the Imperial Crown to bind the British colonies in America; the self-constituted Congress was to be recognised as a taxing and legislative body, on its acknowledgment of the supremacy of the British Legislature; all the recent fiscal and penal legislation was to be repealed, judges were to hold office during good behaviour and not at pleasure, and trial by jury was to be restored.

Had Chatham been in power to carry out some such measure he would probably have succeeded in reconciling for a time all but a small minority in the colonies. But the King, the House of Lords and the ministerialists would have none of it. It was a confession that Great Britain had been wholly in the wrong and that the violations of law and order by the colonists had been justifiable. Above all, the bill recognised Congress, a wholly illegal and revolutionary body, as a lawful organ of authority. The House of Lords refused it even a first reading, and not without more than one personal insult to Chatham himself. Burke's proposals of March 22nd for "reconciliation" met with a similar fate.

And then Chatham once again collapsed. From March 1775 until May 1777, two fateful years, he was out of action,

---

Franklin for a breach of trust and called him a traitor and a thief without protest from the Council—making an administrative indiscretion a major political issue. Had our Government been wiser they could, after censuring Franklin for a breach of trust, have used his argument with great effect. Franklin was dismissed from his post of deputy Postmaster-General, and he returned to Philadelphia convinced that his aim and policy of keeping the colonists loyal within the Empire had failed. Wedderburn's violent language not only turned a serious indiscretion into conduct equivalent to high treason, but the most influential American into an irreconcilable enemy.

seriously ill and at times mentally incapable. Lady Chatham had not only to nurse and comfort a very sick husband, but wrestle with financial difficulties, caused by that husband's reckless extravagance, with the education of her children and her own peevish and intractable brothers. And she accomplished her task in serene and dignified silence, but also with invaluable help from the able and experienced Thomas Coutts, who brought some order into Chatham's disordered finances.

6. The Last Phase: 1775–1778

Two months after the rejection of Chatham's bill there occurred (April 19th) at Lexington the first real clash between the forces of the Crown and armed "colonials," followed by Paul Revere's historic ride through the night across the Charles river to call out "the minute gun" men for the defence of their "liberties." The Civil War had begun, and as Sam Adams expressed it, "what a glorious morning is this."

So little was the gravity of the situation grasped that London was far more interested in "a race of boats called a regatta" and in the trial, "finer than a coronation," of the Duchess of Kingston for bigamy, than in America. And the young ladies of Mayfair discussed with each other and with their mothers whether a young woman of birth and breeding could attend the fashionable spectacle without injury to her morals.

Under the inflexible leadership of the King, the ministry, with the full support of both Houses of Parliament and a majority of the political nation in Great Britain, was determined to crush "rebellion" and to teach these insufferable "colonials" obedience to the law. The Prime Minister, North, alone in the Cabinet had serious misgivings alike as to the policy and the adequacy of the means for enforcing it. But unable to resist his sovereign's personal appeal not to "desert" him, North stayed on, with a heavy heart, for he had no constructive alternative to coercion and little faith in ministerial measures.

The true indictment of ministerial policy from 1768 onwards cannot be based on a charge that both at home and in the colonies they were acting illegally and unconstitutionally, and that the King was deliberately subverting a constitutional system to establish a "Tudor absolutism." With the exception of the vote substituting Luttrell for Wilkes as member for Middlesex, in all the other domestic issues there was a strong case, supported by some of the best legal minds, such as Mansfield, for the "legality" of what was done; and, as has been pointed out, the King in 1760 took over an administrative system from Newcastle and the Whigs, and worked it on strictly customary lines and practice most efficiently to support the ministers whom he appointed to be his "servants." Similarly, in the colonies the "Unitarians" had unquestionably a very strong case for their fundamental principle that the unity of the Empire could only be maintained by accepting and enforcing the right of the Crown in Parliament at Westminster to legislate for the Realm and for the Dominions outside thereunto belonging, and that the distinction between internal and external taxation was untenable in theory and not observed in existing practice. The opposed theory had an equally strong case, and on the purely legal argument one or other had to prevail.

The real indictment of ministerial policy rests on very different grounds. "The Unitarians," like Chatham and the Rockingham Whigs, failed to recognise that the growth of a nation and facts resulting from the growth may make an inherited system invalid and unworkable because the facts and mentality have been completely altered. A remedy can only then be found not in law or custom but in statesmanship and reconstruction. In other words, imagination and insight must be used and a worn-out theory and practice must be adapted to the new situation. The history of the British Empire shows that new wine can be poured into old bottles; but that when a government is determined not only not to repair the old bottles but to go on pouring old wine into them the whole cellar collapses. We today can see that the "old colonial system" had broken down both in theory and in practice: a new system was needed. And if, as seems equally clear, it was impossible either for an eighteenth-century statesman to remodel the inherited fabric or to meet the facts by new measures, it was at least incumbent on statesmanship to ease the cracks and fissures from preventable pressure and, above all, keep those who had to live in the building as contented as possible. Geography, for example, made it impossible to give the colonies direct representation at Westminster; and any such attempt involved a revision of the whole electoral system at home, for which in 1776 not half a dozen votes could have been obtained, and in the half-dozen Burke and the Rockinghams would certainly not have been included.

But the most serious defect in ministerial policy was the supposition that force was a remedy. When the King in the autumn of 1774 wrote that the colonists must either "triumph or submit," did he envisage what "triumph" meant? It could only mean independence by force of arms; and, as the alternative, "submit" to what? Permanent government, on the principle of the Declaratory Act (1766), by force? And for how long could eight millions in Great Britain permanently hold down two millions of "rebels" on a system of government that contradicted the system at home or reconcile them to rule by the Crown in Parliament? The King's sentence was in reality a confession of the bankruptcy not merely of his policy but of the British Empire.

The weakness and defects of the imperial executive in all the thirteen colonies made "coercion" or even the normal administration of the "law" very difficult. These defects have been concisely summed up:[6] "lack of effective imperial control, disunion between the colonies themselves, the weakness of the colonial executive, the means of aggression possessed by colonial elective assemblies, the anomalous position of the judges—secure neither against the executive nor against the legislature—and the unpopularity of admiralty jurisdiction." Rioting and mob violence, which rightly shocked public opinion at home, indicated a deeper moral flaw than the plain

[6] D. L. Keir: *The Constitutional History of Modern Britain*, p. 357.

truth that "coercive measures" were held to be "tyranny" and not law. Owing to the disregard of judicial decisions and the difficulty of enforcing them, the evasion of the Navigation Laws, smuggling and avowed "boot-legging," the conditions on the frontiers where the only law was that of the bowie knife or the tomahawk, and the gnarled individualism in the fibre of most Americans, the thirteen colonies had grown up without any real respect for law or order, unless they suited an individual's case, and this fundamental element in American mentality provided a formidable and continuous problem after 1783.

North's government not only did the wrong thing but they invariably did it, also, in the wrong way. There was in the colonies a strong body of loyalists—"the Tories"—but nothing was done to enlist or organise their support. And the Government at home was both ignorant of the facts and completely misjudged the magnitude and difficulties of the military problem. Lord George Germaine (the Sackville of Minden) was forced to hire Hessians and Hanoverians and Bruns-campaign." After 1768 the home army had been allowed to degenerate in numbers and equipment so that the Government was forced to hire Hessians and Hanoverians and Brunswickers to coerce British subjects in a civil war; recourse was had even to Red Indians. Sandwich at the Admiralty let the Navy down both in numbers and quality; the dockyards were by-words for corruption, graft and inefficiency, and the French were surpassing us in superiority of design and adequacy of material. Nor did the Government grasp the complexity and enormous scale of the theatre of war from the frontiers of Canada to Florida and the size of the forces required for military success. Carleton had strongly recommended a plan which, using Quebec as a northern and New York as a southern base, would have isolated New York State and Massachusetts—the most formidable centres of "rebellion"—from Virginia and Pennsylvania which could then have been "reduced," but Carleton was discarded. Amherst, who really knew what a campaign in these vast spaces involved, refused to serve, and Clive, who might have doubled his military reputation in America, had committed suicide in 1774. "Our army," pronounced a contemporary authority, "will be destroyed by damned driblets," as proved to be the case.

But Clinton put his finger on the gravest feature of ministerial ineptitude when he said: "unless we are sure of a permanent superiority, I tremble for the fatal consequences at sea." In plain fact, without the command of the sea war with the "rebels" could only end in humiliating failure. And it did. The Bourbon powers, as Chatham predicted, were the danger. Ministerial policy was driving "the colonials" into finding a strong ally: since 1763 it was a common belief that France would welcome a war of revenge and it was known that much had been done to reorganise both her fleet and her army. Her neutrality would depend not on British foreign policy but on her estimate of British strength and on what happened in North America. And at Versailles in 1775, 1776 and 1777 they were very well informed about both.

Event followed event with the inevitability of a Greek tragedy. A timid conciliation proposal of North (March 1775) was rejected by Congress as "unreasonable and insidious," and, on strictly constitutional lines, a Petition to the King was adopted (July 8th, 1775) appealing from the Crown in Parliament to the Crown as sovereign in the dominions outside the Realm, the author of their rights as subjects and the guardian of those rights to self-government as laid down in the various Royal Charters as against their violation by ministers illegally using statutes outside the powers of Parliament. The Crown was requested to find "some mode" for restoring by its prerogative authority a lawful settlement. In other words, a large body of British subjects was claiming "Dominion Status" within the Empire. It was the colonials' last offer for "reconciliation," but before it was rejected (September 1st) the King by an Order in Council (August 23rd) had declared the North American colonies to be in a "state of rebellion," and in December all trade with the rebels was prohibited by statute. The constitutional phase of the controversy was ended. The Civil War had begun.

The next phase was inevitably and logically revolutionary in the proper sense of that term. The famous Declaration of Independence of July 4th, 1776, was an appeal to the world in language and for reasons intelligible to all and sundry. Independence was claimed, not merely redress against the illegal action of a Crown in a legislature assuming a jurisdiction it had not got, or against a sovereign abusing the prerogative which in law he possessed, but by free men and women whom no authority could deprive of their rights as human beings, natural and inalienable and part of a divine order and system and government of the universe. The drafting of this historic document was mainly the work of Jefferson, but through it run the ideas of Paine, who had gone to America in 1774, and whose pamphlets and *Common Sense* (1776) exercised an immense influence on American thought. Political theory had now ousted constitutional law, however interpreted, as the basis of the controversy.

It is no doubt useless to speculate on what might have happened had Chatham's bill for conciliation been accepted. It might have led gradually to a "mode of government" approximate to that reached by very different roads and by many stages as defined in the Statute of Westminster a hundred and fifty years later. But in 1775 the ministerialists were in such overwhelming command and so deep was the antagonism in sentiment and the distrust on both sides of the Atlantic that the only solution of the imperial problem was either in unconditional submission or unconditional victory. In either case the First British Empire ceased to exist.

The opposition in Great Britain was impotent, for its name, as Horace Walpole rightly said, was "anarchy." The handful who followed Chatham, including the able Shelburne who had unhappily forfeited the confidence of everyone but himself, differed from the larger body of "the Rockinghams" who, like Burke and Adam Smith, no longer regarded the Navigation and Trades Laws as the essentials of an imperial system and were slowly being convinced that the only way out of a perilous situation was to grant the demand for independence and concentrate on the war, now at hand, with France and probably Spain also. But even a unified opposition would have failed to shake the real Prime Minister, the King, whose inflexible obstinacy alone prevented North from throwing in his hand.

When Chatham at last, on May 30th, 1777, with a mind once again clear and a shattered body, reappeared in London he found public opinion gravely alarmed. American resistance was proving more formidable and successful than the ignorant optimists, like Germaine, had predicted: "the rebels" in Congress were appealing to France for aid, and to those who remembered 1756–57 "the precious go-cart" (to use Pitt's phrase) was again most unpleasantly nearing the edge of a precipice. One man and one man only could save them— William Pitt, now Earl of Chatham. The last phase of nine months began in June 1777; and the sun of his genius set in majestic splendour. "He was never so great," wrote a contemporary, "as when abandoned by all." For abandoned he was, despite the rising surge in public opinion to call him to office to direct the ship of state. To North's doubting bleats the King made it clear that "no consideration in life shall make me stoop to opposition," not even when in December the news arrived that on October 17th Burgoyne, ambushed and surrounded, had capitulated to "the rebels" at Saratoga. The disaster was as much the fault of Germaine as of Burgoyne, for he had failed to send the necessary instructions to Howe, whose forces were to be an integral part of the enveloping movement—failed apparently because Germaine, due to go into the country, "would not keep his horses waiting in the street."

Saratoga was much more than a disagreeable defeat. It brought France in. Vergennes was at last satisfied that the Americans would not leave an ally in the lurch either by submission or defeat. Franklin and Deane had reached Paris from Congress, and on February 6th, 1778, an alliance between the "rebels" and France was signed, one condition of which was that the war would continue until independence had been gained. Franklin could now brush his brown suit. It would surely not be long before he could put it on.

Chatham's last effort to save the Empire a second time was made in five great speeches (May 30th, November 20th, December 2nd, December 5th and December 11th, 1777), the main points in which simply repeated with burning conviction and unforgettable phrase his English and imperial creed. Our policy since 1764 had been wholly wrong, "the pursuit of a peppercorn," by violation of plain constitutional rights; we had driven loyal subjects to resistance in defence of their liberties, and they were right to resist; by measure upon measure we had united our fellow-subjects in their opposition, and now we talked idly of conquering them; that would prove to be impossible, even if we "trafficked and bartered with every little pitiful German prince that sends and sells his subjects to the shambles of a foreign ruler"; and while we were engaged in this continuity of blunder we forgot that French intervention hung over us by "a slender and brittle thread," and in a matter of internal policy we could not venture to tell the Court of Versailles that we would not tolerate the presence of American plenipotentiaries inviting the interference of a foreign and neutral power in a domestic dispute; and, worst of all, we were wholly unprepared to take up the challenge from Versailles, with England and Ireland denuded for an ignominious war in America.

It was an unanswerable indictment; and on one point Chatham remained unshaken—the disruption of the Empire by granting independence. "I will," he informed Shelburne, "as soon subscribe to Transubstantiation as to sovereignty (by right) in the colonies." The scales at last were falling off the eyes of a people bemused by ministerial mediocrity; the nation was demanding Chatham and, as Grenville noted of Peel in 1846, "all eyes are turned upon him as if by a sort of fascination," though the contemporary record of 1777 is stained with the vulgar spite of some peers and commoners deriding "a vain old dotard with a short memory." It is perhaps possible that, had Chatham, even in January 1778, been called to power the magic of his prestige and the trust in his sincerity might have halted the Revolution by his proposal to withdraw our troops from the American continent with a renewal of the terms, outlined in his bill of 1775, and proposed in the Petition of Congress of July in that year. This would have given the colonies a real autonomy and kept them at any rate for a time within the jurisdiction and sovereignty of the Crown. But the tattered sibylline books were not on offer in January 1778. The King categorically refused either to see Chatham or personally to negotiate with him. Chatham was a broken man, and after the signature of the alliance with France on February 6th, there was nothing to do but to fight it out.

Nevertheless North, as usual too late, made the effort. On February 17th the serried phalanx of ministerialists and King's Friends listened in silent consternation to the Prime Minister's exposition of "terms of conciliation" which practically admitted that the Government had been wholly in the wrong since 1769, and offered what amounted to submission to the demands (short of independence) of these damnable "rebels." "Such a bundle of imbecility," observed the stout Tory, Dr. Johnson, "never disgraced a nation." But what the colonists might have taken from Chatham they were not prepared to discuss with North or his commissioners, whose good faith and sudden conversion they regarded as subtle moves in the plan of men determined to enslave them and to rivet the fetters more securely on men determined to be free.

The Rockinghams had definitely split with Chatham, who, ill and feeble, heard with "unspeakable concern" that the young Duke of Richmond was moving on April 7th a motion requesting the King to dismiss his ministers, withdraw his troops and negotiate with the Americans, "to recover their friendship at heart, if not their allegiance"; he was determined to attend and oppose. When, supported by his son, William, and his son-in-law, Lord Mahon, he entered the House, with his shrunken frame but with eyes still lit by their paralysing brilliance, the assembly rose in respectful greeting. Voice and words faltered when he came to speak, leaning heavily on his crutches. But some immortal sentences rang out: "shall a people that fifteen years ago was the terror of the world now stoop so low as to tell its ancient inveterate foe: 'take all we have, only give us peace': . . . my Lords, any state is better than despair: if we must fall, let us fall like men." Half an hour later, attempting to rise and reply, he collapsed on his seat. In the dismayed Chamber, with peers running here and there for help, for cordials, for water, for doctors, Mansfield alone remained absolutely unmoved. Chatham was presently carried out, rallied and two days later was driven to his residence, Hayes. Another rally, and then the end came on May 11th.

In the Commons North supported the motion for a public funeral and a monument at the public charge in Westminster Abbey; but the Peers by a casting vote refused to attend as a body, and the Lord Chancellor, the Archbishop of York and two other peers (Chandos and Paget) signalised themselves by entering a Protest against a funeral and monument at the public expense. More notable and characteristic, the King registered his regret at "the vote" as "an offensive measure to me personally." But to the public Chatham remained the Great Commoner; and after lying in state in the Painted Chamber (June 7th and 8th) the funeral procession, in all pomp and ceremony, passed through the homage of a great multitude to the tomb by the North Door of the Abbey. And there today, with two other tombs fitly added—Hester Grenville Pitt "his beloved wife," and the second and younger William Pitt, the Pilot who weathered the storm—English and Americans can stand and pay their silent tribute to a statesman whose ideals and achievement are the common heritage of the British Empire and the United States of America.

Epilogue

Epilogue

CHATHAM'S CAREER is unique in our political annals, at least since 1689. Every political leader of the first class for two and a half centuries has been a member and then a leader of a powerful and organised party. Walpole, the younger Pitt, Fox, Canning, Peel, Palmerston, Disraeli, Gladstone, Balfour, Joseph Chamberlain, Asquith, Lloyd George—we can only envisage and think of as foremost figures whose strength was based and buttressed on a large group of followers united by a recognisable and common creed and programme to which their head strove to give expression in policy, action and legislation. But while it would be absurd and unhistorical to expect a party led by Chatham to be a party in the nineteenth-century sense of the term, it struck his contemporaries as forcibly as it does us today that Pitt had no "connection," "group" or "faction" to follow him into office, or to make opposition by him formidable.

And this feature of his career was not due to lack of opportunity or persons who could have been cemented and organised as the eighteenth century understood "party." In this respect his career is a continually shifting kaleidoscope; he worked with many groups from 1735 when he entered Parliament and was reckoned to be one of "Cobham's Cubs," but he never worked long, and he invariably broke with each, if it did not first break with him—with "the Cobhamites," with

133

the Grenvilles, with Leicester House, with "the Newcastles," with "the Bedfords," with "the Rockinghams." For with Chatham his independence was a feature of his character and a principle of his political creed. He could not "bear the slightest touch of command," and he could say with truth: "I myself am one of the people—by birth an English elector, I join with the freeholders of England as in a common cause . . . an administration formed upon an exclusive system of family connections or private friendships cannot be long supported in this country . . . no single man's private friendships or connections are sufficient to form or overturn an administration." For the methods and technique by which a "party" could be made and kept together he had neither taste nor aptitude. Politics were an affair of large and invigorating issues for large and invigorating ends. Peerages, pensions, places of profit, ribbons, decorations—the gewgaws and toys by which men are cajoled or bribed—let those who dabbled and trafficked in such do so, for it was probably all they were fit to do.

Chatham in fact is the only great figure who reached high office not in spite of, but because of, his independence. And because there has never again been a second Chatham there has never been an independent to repeat his record. And with his independence is linked his disregard, amounting to contempt, for consistency. Other great statesmen have deliberately changed from one party to another, admitting that they had changed; but Chatham could denounce and indict a Walpole, a Carteret or a Newcastle as public enemies and presently proclaim without a syllable of penitence or the quiver of an eyelid that they were either great men or capable administrators who had served their country well and from whom he and all could learn much. He could blast the electorate of Hanover with the lava of denunciation, and the Elbe as an ocean of gore, and presently send a hundred thousand men to protect it and claim that he had won Canada in Germany. For instinctively he knew that his countrymen cared as little for consistency as he did; for the sneers or jeers of the lobby at Westminster or White's Club they, as he, reckoned nothing. Results were a greater virtue in statesmanship than adherence to a worn-out principle or article of faith, and Chatham either gave them results or made them realise the gravity and significance of his attitude in controversy. He never took part in a controversy without adding to its dignity or infusing into it some vital bearing on the higher elements in the national destinies.

One of the most difficult but unquestionable facts to explain is how he became the idol of a nation. Of his powers of speech the evidence of those who heard him—and many were fastidious critics such as Horace Walpole and Grattan—is unanimous and complete. Figure, voice, gesture, language combined to put him in a class by himself; few if any could face the eyes that "could cut a diamond," and able men and no mean debaters such as Murray (Mansfield) "cowered" under the lash of that terrible tongue. But speeches were not reported even as they were in the days of his son and Charles Fox, and those who heard him were very limited in number. Nor can any speech, however carefully reported, have the effect of the spoken word: for great oratory is dependent on the day, hour and atmosphere of the situation and on the inexplicable wave-length that links a speaker with his audience. Have we all not been deeply moved by a speech, whether in a hall or a pulpit, and next day wondered, when we read the same words in print, how and why we had been so moved? Oratory perishes with the utterance, but the orator does not, for the enchanter may by his personality cast a deeper and more durable spell than the wand of his enchantment. And here again we wrestle with the mystery of personality. Some great orators only impress when and so long as they speak; the words have wings for the hour but the speaker evaporates even more quickly than what he says; but with a very select few, spell-binding as may be the words, behind and through them is an inexplicable force—a personality penetrating through to other personalities—and stamping a quality of imprint that neither time nor human frailty can obliterate. It was to this very small class that Chatham belonged. The man was greater than the magic of his voice, gesture and words. Everyone who heard him felt it in the core of his being. And this uplifting of the spirit remained to steel and quicken.

But this does not explain his power over those who never heard or even saw him, those outside the House of Commons whose sense, as George II said, he taught authority to recognise. Chatham never represented a constituency with more than a hunderd votes; he never made speeches in those constituencies with their handful of voters, nor did he ever outside Westminster address such an audience as Burke did at Bristol, or Wilkes in Middlesex; he was the idol of the City of London, but he did not harangue either Aldermen, Freemen or the mob; the Midlothian campaign of a Gladstone was as much out of the question as a flight in an aeroplane. Yet on a resignation it could "rain gold boxes," while his influence in the North American colonies, three thousand miles away, where his name was a household word, is still more mysterious. It is not a case of a reputation made by the printed word, by Fleet Street and journalists stamping an interpretation through skilful pens and printer's ink on millions at least able to read, who then by some alchemy transmute what they read into a mental reality, influencing conduct. We can only infer that eighteenth-century England was like Central Africa or large areas in India and China, where an idea, a belief, a conviction, a rumour, started by a few with first-hand experience, spreads with the speed of light and grips thousands because it harmonises with conscious or inarticulate and subconscious aspirations, hopes and fears. No one in Chatham's lifetime except himself was such a national force and idol; had a plebiscite been possible he would not have been forced to resign in 1761 and he would have been put back into power in 1769. Had he lived four centuries earlier, miracles would have taken place at his tomb. For Chatham was and remained unique.

This impression of power—$\delta\alpha\iota\mu\acute{o}\nu\iota\nu\nu$ $\tau\acute{\iota}$—was universal, and as strong with those who disliked or hated the part he was playing as with those who enthusiastically welcomed it. And foreigners felt it as deeply as his countrymen. Choiseul, for example, never met Chatham, but he feared him more than any other living human being; and in 1775 the one anxiety of Vergennes and the Court of Versailles was that the man of 1757 might be recalled to supreme authority. A contemporary critic noted of Mrs. Siddons that in a tragedy at Drury Lane when she appeared under a large archway she seemed to fill it. Chatham always filled the archway, and the larger the archway the more he filled it.

Did his contemporaries ever see the real Chatham, or, putting the question in another way, was there another Chatham behind the imposing figure who invariably was in full dress, unbending, stately, dignified, haughty, and at times intolerably arrogant? The evidence is conflicting because the recorders of it were themselves puzzled. Many were sincerely convinced that the man was a superb *poseur,* an actor from start to finish, aiming always at effect and not infrequently stooping to the tricks of the charlatan; that his gout and swathings of flannel, the crutches in velvet and the huge periwig were part of his technique, and that in his physical sufferings he often came near to being a malingerer. No final or conclusive verdict can ever be pronounced, for Chatham, like Cromwell, will always be interpreted by the personal, if unconscious, bias of the interpreter. But to the present writer three things seem clear.

First, Chatham himself took life and himself with great seriousness, and with very little sense of humour (as distinct from irony and sarcasm) saw every occasion and situation, as the great actor does, as a dramatic moment with which his personal feeling must fit in. He was playing a part in that sense, but the circumstances were such as to require an attitude both in words and behaviour that would impress his audience, small or great, with the same intensity of conviction that he himself was feeling. This trait of temperament slowly and unconsciously crystallised into a habit, which became as natural to himself as it might be puzzling to everyone else.

Secondly, the evidence for this domestic or private life is **most** regrettably scanty. Pompous letters about the English scene, nymphs and groves, pur'ing rills and dryads of the woods were part of the idiom of the eighteenth century, and they did not strike their readers as artificial or hollow bombast. The young heroes and heroines of Scott and Jane Austen (a good deal later) talk to each other in a way that astonishes us today, but the readers found such conversation perfectly natural, for they talked like that themselves; and a study of Goldsmith, Sheridan and Dodsley's collection of plays confirms the conclusion. There is, also, fragmentary evidence in letters between Hester Grenville and himself, expressed in words of simple and deep affection, which seem to lift a curtain and provide a peep, at any rate, into a life which only Chatham and his family knew. When Lady Chatham and her children went to the seaside, coaches and a retinue of liveried domestics, male and female, were absolutely necessary, for they were a sign of status to which Chatham (and not alone in his world) attached serious importance. But today we should indeed rub our eyes if we saw the Treasury Bench in either House occupied by men in full court dress, with their stars and ribbons, or read an apology to a Duke for an unintentional discourtesy because on a summer day he was not wearing his ribbon of the Garter when on horseback in his own park. Chatham, it is fairly certain, in his private life, teaching the young William to translate Demosthenes into good English, was not the Chatham that the world saw, but pride, if nothing else, dropped the curtain, as it has always dropped it on our sovereigns when they retire to their private apartments.

Thirdly, much allowance must be made for the physical handicaps that oppressed Chatham since his boyhood at Eton. His "gout" is really part of our national history and it seems certain that he never enjoyed normal health for twelve continuous months in the whole of his life. That he lived to the age of seventy is a proof of the power and quality of his spirit, for most men would have ceased to strive with physical difficulties so crippling and depressing: and he had to wrestle with much more than "gout." Emotional instability, irritability, racked nerves, megalomaniac fancies and ambition, arrogance—all these and much else would be intelligible to the medical expert today as neuroses, pointing to a graver malady; to the medical science of the eighteenth century they were unintelligible or misinterpreted. But Chatham's incurable financial extravagance, his inability to square income with expenditure, his lavish spending on buildings, gardens and forestry are unquestionably linked up with his haughty pride and passion for external magnificence in house and staff; they are psychological elements in a morbid pathology, and the difficulty is to assign to them their precise share in the less attractive sides of his character.

We must not forget that in one feature he remained consistent and justifiably proud. As a young man his letters show that he could "romp with the girls" and take a full part in the frolics (not always in the best of taste) of the patrician mansions where he was a welcome guest. But neither before nor after his marriage could the most malignant lampooner throw one stone or one flick of mud at his domestic and private life as they could and did at most of his relatives and his contemporaries. No "chargeable ladies" or illegitimate children were responsible for his embarrassed finances. To Hester Grenville he brought a single-hearted devotion. Both on his and her tomb the superb line of Propertius could have been engraved:

Viximus insignes inter utramque facem:

(Between the torch of marriage and of death our life has been noble).

These and other points, of which too often too much has been made, are only significant if they help to a correct valuation of his place in our national record and development. In many periods of history we can feel with some justification that if this or that prominent figure had been removed or never played out his part the course of events would not have been so materially different, because either things would of themselves have gone as they did or some other person would have filled the gap; but just as we cannot imagine the seventeenth century without Cromwell or any substitute for Cromwell, we cannot imagine the eighteenth century without Chatham or fix on any one of his contemporaries as a substitute. And we dislocate the focus if we regard him simply as the greatest war minister in our annals: for Chatham was much more than that.

Two qualities in his political life stand out not only for their part in shaping the evolution and character of his period, but for an abiding influence after his death. With the exception of Cromwell, he was the most English in his nationalism of all our statesmen; the Empire was for him as powerful a vision and inspiration of conduct as the ideal of heaven to the true saint.

Through all his political life, with its demonstrable inconsistencies in method or tactics, runs a unifying red thread. Is this policy, this proposal, this objective really English? Not once but a dozen times in successive crises rings the insistent question: "are these measures English?" That for Chatham was the test: and the answer could reconcile or dismiss inconsistencies, because a truly English interest would necessarily vary with each situation and its needs. And this "Englishry" as the supreme element in statesmanship was indissolubly bound up with, and flowed from, his interpretation of the Empire and Imperial policy. For the Empire, as for the homeland, meant that every English boy and girl was born into an inheritance which had, like Chatham's reverence for the Crown, the symbol and organ of unified sentiment and authority, a mystical element. Chatham desired power, trade and prosperity—they were both ends and instruments of policy—but the Empire was something higher, deeper and more rewarding than power, trade and prosperity. We had as Englishmen our birthright of inalienable liberties, whether we lived in Fountain Court or Mayfair, or Boston or the Mosquito coast; to limit this birthright for any group of our blood or speech was not only "tyranny" but a blow at all the others, apparently unaffected perhaps by the action. The freedom we inherited was as necessary as the air we breathed; to deny it was to stifle and fetter, and so deprive life of some of its essential values. For to be an Englishman conferred a right, and, also, a duty to a way of life better than any material privileges that citizenship conferred.

Defeat by France in 1757 or 1777 was not merely humiliating or impoverishing; it meant that in two great hemispheres the men of our race would not be able to establish across the seas the England to which they belonged or live the life that was their right in the Divine order of things. A France dominant on the continent of Europe, in North America and Hindustan was a denial of all that the Empire stood for and guaranteed to every one of its members. France, therefore, must be defeated. It was an imperative English interest, which it was treason to ignore or surrender.

Chatham accepted the Empire as he found it in 1735; he did not see that by 1760 the structure had decayed, that the principles on which that structure rested had lost their efficacy, and that an organic reconstruction was essential. Such an analysis as made Adam Smith's *Wealth of Nations* (published in 1776, the year of the Declaration of Independence) memorable was written in language that he could not understand. And, as has been previously pointed out, the principles of his American policy did not really meet the fundamentals of the imperial problem, or provide the basis for a durable settlement. But had he been allowed to handle matters after 1763, or had his proposals even as late as 1774 been put into execution by himself, the crisis would either never have arisen or would have been bridged over, and Great Britain would have avoided a disastrous civil war, while France would have been made to understand that her intervention would cost her more than she had paid in 1763.

There would have been no "intervention." For the supreme quality of Chatham's statesmanship lay in his intuition and conviction that in the larger issues governments and policy are not affairs of law, as lawyers might interpret it, or of material measures, but of minds dealing with minds. The true statesman was one who could inspire every man and woman with the same conviction and springs of conduct as inspired himself. And if friction or grievances threatened the harmony or balance of life in the Commonwealth, the diagnosis and the remedy must be psychological or mental. To Chatham the "Americans" were not "Colonials" or Americans; they were Englishmen of the same fibre and temper as himself; they were not "subjects," they were fellow-citizens and they had a right to demand precisely the treatment that every citizen in the homeland expected. The "Stamp Act" raised precisely the same issue as the taxation without the consent of Parliament, which led to the Great Rebellion in 1641, and the colonists were *right* to resist. That it was their duty to contribute to imperial defence was as obvious as was the duty of an Englishman in Middlesex or Wiltshire, but if the contribution was to be by "internal" taxation then it must be by free consent through the appropriate legislature: punishment for resistance by suppressing that legislature was "tyranny"; the use of Hessians to enforce "order" was as hateful as to use them to shoot on a "mob" at Temple Bar; and a government that could employ such means for such purposes was destroying the title-deeds not merely of "colonists" but of all Englishmen.

Chatham, therefore, saw in the constitutional controversies at home the same issues that had been raised at Boston or Philadelphia. Even as late as 1775 his bill, so contemptuously rejected in the House of Lords, might have saved the situation, as Franklin thought; though he did not see that his proposals really undermined his own position, resting on an untenable maintenance of "external" taxation. But that bill really contained the seeds of "Dominion Status," which would have slowly and irresistibly germinated.

What was even of more importance at the moment, the tightening deadlock was a question of confidence. For nations —and the colonists unconsciously had almost become a nation—are always like fine pedigree racehorses, "delicate feeders": they will refuse from one hand precisely the food that they will readily accept from another. The Americans trusted Chatham; but the Danai—a Grenville, a North, a Hillsborough or a George III—were feared even when they offered welcome gifts. Only too often in any period of history the greatest difficulty for the historian is not the lack of a manuscript which can be cited as proof, but the reconstruction of the atmosphere and mental forces moving powerful individuals and groups or masses. An hour's talk with Chatham, Junius, North or Germaine, with Franklin, Otis, Jefferson or either of the Adams, would be more illuminating than a bundle of unpublished despatches or letters.

And as with America so with India. To Chatham corruption, bribery, profiteering and all the "abuses which stank to Heaven" were hateful because they were the degradation of a true English character; but when the East India Company was transformed by a Clive from a purely trading company into an organ of government Chatham grasped that a wholly new and complex problem confronted the British people. Indians, alike in Bengal, Orissa or the Carnatic, had ceased to be foreigners with whom we traded by treaty or contract and had been admitted into the imperial system. How were we to discharge the responsibility now imposed on us, how in return for the rights so acquired were they to discharge the duties now imposed on them? That could not be answered simply by referring to a terminable charter, granted and defined under a wholly different situation. It must, therefore, have been a shock when Chatham declared that "the affections of Bengal" were more important than dividends and profitable trade, sharper than when he avowed his friendship and obligations to Franklin, whom a Wedderburn had with the assent of his colleagues openly insulted at the Privy Council.

And it is one of the lamentable lost opportunities when Chatham's physical collapse failed to prevent not only Charles Townshend's blunder in colonial taxation but also his equally unhappy dealings with the East India Company, which successfully evaded the real issues and bartered rights inherent in the Crown for a mess of pottage. Fate did not allow Chatham a second opportunity, and North's timid Regulating Act of 1773 did either too little or too much, as the career of Warren Hastings proved up to the hilt.

On India, as on Parliamentary Reform, Chatham in fact showed a deeper insight into the nature of the problem, and a clearer grip on the right remedy, than Burke, who thought that the Ten Tables from an imaginary Sinai in 1689 provided an irrefutable answer to all the questions of each succeeding generation. And it was from his father and not from the old Whigs that the second William Pitt, born in the year of victory, 1759, learned, with reverence for the teacher, principles that were to make both a new Whig and a new Tory party. In one respect alone Chatham was happy in the opportunity of his death; for he was spared from living through blunder and disaster to the surrender of York Town, spared from the bitter fulfilment of his prediction that "you cannot conquer the Americans," spared from defeat by France, and from the disruption of the Empire. And those living in 1783 could realise that if William Pitt had been right in 1757 he had been still more superbly right from 1763 to 1778, which was not the true end. For since a dying man was carried out from the House of Lords each succeeding generation has felt that Chatham's spirit is immortal and has its message to all of English speech:

> The nature of our people,
> Our city's institutions and the terms
> For common justice, you're as pregnant in
> As art and practice hath enrichèd any
> That we remember . . .
> There is a kind of character in thy life
> That, to th' observer, doth thy history
> Fully unfold.

Appendix I

Chatham's Connections

WHEN Horace Walpole and other contemporary writers speak of Pitt's lack of "connections" they use the term in its political sense. In its more ordinary sense he was connected with seven separate peerages:

1. The Strathfieldsaye Pitts (of Encombe), who obtained the Barony of Rivers in 1722, which lasted to 1828 and was continued by special remainder to W. Beckford.
2. The Barony of Camelford, through the son of his brother Thomas (married to Christian Lyttelton), who became the first Lord Camelford of Boconnoc in 1784.
3. The Earldom of Londonderry, by his uncle, Thomas Pitt (son of Governor and "Diamond" Pitt), who became the first Baron in 1719, advanced to an earldom in 1726. The title became extinct in 1765—on the death of the third earl without issue.
4. The Earls Stanhope: (doubly) by (1) his Aunt Lucy, who married the first Earl Stanhope; (2) her grandson, the third Earl, married Chatham's daughter, Hester, and was mother of the notable Lady Hester, niece of the younger (William) Pitt.
5. The Temple-Grenvilles—by his marriage to Hester Grenville, sister to Earl Temple and George Grenville, and so (through him) to the Marquis and Duke of Buckingham

and to Baron Grenville, nephews of his wife Hester,
Lady Chatham.

6. Lord Grenville, who married Anne Pitt, daughter of the
   first, and sister of the second, Lord Camelford.

7. Lord Lyttelton (of Hagley), by his brother Thomas, who
   married Christian Lyttelton, sister of the first Baron
   and mother of the first Lord Camelford.

The earldom of Chatham conferred on William Pitt in 1766
became extinct in 1835, on the death of the second earl, John
Pitt, without issue.

Appendix II

Books on Chatham

THE STANDARD *Life* is by Prof. Basil Williams, in 2 vols., superseding all previous biographies; this can be supplemented by Brian Tunstall, *William Pitt, Earl of Chatham* (1 vol., 1938).

These two biographies contain full bibliographies of the original MS. and printed sources.

The Life of Chatham, by Albert von Ruville (Eng. transl. in 3 vols., 1907), contains some information from Prussian archives; but as an expert, Sir R. Lodge, has expressed it, the judgments on Chatham's public and personal life are "fantastic," though worked out with perverse German ingenuity.

To these must be added as indispensable:

L. B. NAMIER: *Structure of Politics at the Accession of George III* (2 vols.), 1929. *England in the Age of the American Revolution*, 1930.

ROMNEY SEDGWICK: *Letters of Lord Bute and George III*, with a valuable introduction by the Editor.

Sir JULIAN CORBETT: *England in the Seven Years War* (2 vols.), 1907.

KATE HOTBLACK: *Chatham's Colonial Policy*, 1917.

Sir J. W. FORTESCUE: *Correspondence of George III* (in 6 vols., the first four of which cover the period from 1760–1778), unfortunately badly edited.

The best introduction to the American and Colonial history is vol. 1 of *The Cambridge History of the British Empire* (with full bibliographies to each chapter or section).

The American Revolution, an illuminating study of the constitutional and legal principles, by a high authority, Prof. H. C. MacIlwain.

On the War of the Austrian Succession and the relations of Great Britain and Prussia between 1740 and 1760: see particularly:

Sir R. LODGE: *Great Britain and Prussia in the Eighteenth Century* (1922), and *Studies in Eighteenth-century Diplomacy* (1929); and on the relations of Great Britain and Hanover:

Sir A. WARD: *Great Britain and Hanover,* 1899.

To understand the imperial problems of Chatham's day, and his contribution to their solution, a study of the historical geography of four areas is essential. (1) Central Europe— Hanover, Prussia and the dynastic territories of the House of Habsburg, together with the accesses by sea from Great Britain to the Continent and the Mediterranean. (2) North America, including the West Indies. (3) The Atlantic strategic field, including West Africa. (4) The peninsula of Hindustan and the approaches to it by sea from the Cape of Good Hope.

Index

Index

There are no references in this Index to William Pitt, 1st Earl of Chatham, because it would involve an indication to almost every page. The chief phases of his career are set out, with dates, in the Table of Contents.